What people are saying about it.

The **Brand** *of* **You**

The ultimate guide
for an interior designer's
career journey

The
Brand
of
You

The ultimate guide
for an interior designer's
career journey

Aga Artka & Jenny Rebholz

Henschel
HAUS
publishing, Inc.
Milwaukee, Wisconsin

Updated edition August 2016
Illustrations/maps by Aga Artka

Published by
HenschelHAUS Publishing, Inc.
www.henschelHAUSbooks.com

Please contact the publisher
for information on academic
or non-profit quantity discounts.

ISBN: 978-1-59598-435-7
LCCN: 2015952247
CIP: PENDING

Copy and Developmental editing by Jessie Dowd
Proofreading by HenschelHAUS Publishing, Inc.
Book design, layout, and cover design by Wendi Van Eldik
Author photographs by ©Tricia Shay Photography

Publisher's Cataloging-In-Publication Data
(Prepared by The Donohue Group, Inc.)

Artka, Aga.
The Brand of You: The ultimate guide for an interior designer's career journey
Aga Artka & Jenny Rebholz.

pages: illustrations; cm

Includes bibliographical references.
ISBN: 978-1-59598-435-7

1. Interior decoration–Vocational guidance. 2. Interior decoration–Practice.
3. Artka, Aga–Career in interior decoration. 4. Rebholz, Jenny–Career in
interior decoration. I. Rebholz, Jenny. II. Title.

NK2116 .A78 2016
747.023   2015952247
Printed in the United States of America

If this book helps one person, it is a success.

CONTENTS ━━━━━━▶

FOREWORD ⟶

H AVE YOU EVER been killing time in a crowded café, secretively observing the people around you, and wondered if...The woman talking on the headset two tables over is the CEO of a start-up luxury LED lighting company? The man madly typing on his laptop is the hiring manager at a prominent architecture and design firm? The teenager wearing headphones and casually doodling in her journal will be on the cover of *Metropolis* magazine in 10 years for her innovative and eco-friendly textile manufacturing techniques?

If you have, then you are probably in the interior design industry–or you want to be–and it is a very good thing that you picked up this book.

Think about it: No one knows who you are, what you do or what you are capable of until you tell them, show them or otherwise convince them, and it is quite possible that at some point, those three people in the café each gazed over at you and wondered if you were the designer of her company's first award-winning collection? Or perhaps the next project manager of his firm's healthcare project team, or the future business partner who inspires her to dream bigger than she ever believed she could?

Until someone invents a technology allowing us to view a person's resume simply by looking in his or her direction, we must make the effort to network and practice promoting ourselves. You can be the most talented person in the world, but if no one knows it, then your gifts will go unnoticed, unappreciated and, ultimately, underutilized, leading to an extremely frustrating career.

During my two decades in the interior design industry, networking has served me very well. When I was enrolled in the interior design graduate program at the Savannah College of Art and Design

(SCAD), I was the only student who ever showed up at local industry events and engaged with professionals. The result: I secured three invaluable internships over the course of two-and-a-half years, providing me insight into what I liked to do and, more importantly, what I didn't.

After graduating, I moved back to Dallas, not knowing a soul in the interior design industry. Fortunately, I arrived just in time for holiday events, and I took advantage of the season. By attending just two cocktail parties, mustering up the courage to introduce myself to a multitude of strangers and telling "my story" as an emerging interior designer, I landed a provisional position at a well-respected hospitality firm and, eventually, a full-time position at a small commercial design firm that turned into a fruitful eight-year run.

When I became restless, I reached out to an acquaintance in the retail industry for advice, because I knew that he had successfully reinvented himself several times over the course of his career. After many questions, a couple glasses of wine and a few hours brainstorming about how I could create some type of informational resource for aspiring interior designers, thereby giving back to the industry that I loved, the idea for plinthandchintz.com was born.

Making the right connections can take you to wonderful and unexpected places, which is further evidenced by the fact that I am writing the foreword to this book. I met authors Jenny Rebholz and Aga Artka through mutual friends I made through my volunteer leadership in American Society of Interior Designers (ASID). Early in the life of *PLiNTH & CHiNTZ*, Jenny began contributing articles that echoed my viewpoint. When she and Aga started collaborating several years later, their co-authored advice on how to advance one's career resonated loudly with me and my readers, and only reinforced the sentiments that I had been communicating to both emerging and established professionals for years. I am beyond thrilled that they have taken the time to expand upon their topics, organize them and publish this book.

In the same vein of Albert Einstein's statement that "genius is 1 percent talent and 99 percent hard work," I wholeheartedly believe that success is 10 percent talent and 90 percent hard work. Living inside their active, creative minds, many designers can be introverts, taking their talents for granted and shielding deep wells of knowledge from potential employers and clients. However, selling your skill sets, ideas and yourself is absolutely crucial to securing future positions and projects, and, ultimately, to the sustainability of your career.

If you cannot stand to think of yourself as a "salesperson," then instead think of yourself as a "promoter of you," and a promoter of the interior design profession and the industry as a whole. The difference is subtle, but that shift in mindset has worked amazingly well for me, and it–along with a great deal of hard work in the form of volunteering, networking, lecturing and writing–has allowed me to establish a positive reputation for myself that serves as my "introduction" before I ever walk through a door, put on a name tag or shake a single hand.

PLiNTH & CHiNTZ, my definitive calling card, has been–and continues to be–a positive platform for me to promote the diversity of opportunities and depth of expertise within the industry, but it has taken years of hard work. The proof? In the last decade, I have shared with readers 600-plus design terms, 800-plus resource links, countless competitions and an endless number of global design events. Between articles that I have written and those submitted by my 150-plus contributors, the count is more than 650 (so far!). This constant collaboration with peers, coupled with my additional role as manager and promoter of METROCON Expo & Conference, the annual multidisciplinary interior design tradeshow and conference in Dallas, has kept me energized and recognized.

Nothing makes me happier than being a connector of people, because I am convinced that the key to success in business, and in life, is about making the right connections, forging those relationships and then nurturing them to be mutually beneficial. Therefore, it brings me especially great joy to help connect you to Jenny and Aga. Jenny is sharp, endlessly curious and open to new paths, and Aga is driven, tireless and positively ebullient. Together, they are a force, and if you follow their advice, the sky is the limit for you and your interior design career.

— Laura McDonald Stewart, *RID, ASID, LEED AP*
Founder/Editor, PLiNTH & CHiNTZ,
The Online Interior Design Magazine
Manager/Promoter, METROCON Expo
& Conference-Dallas

PREFACE → *Jenny*

THERE IS A starting point for everything, right? The moment when the seed is planted. The same goes for this book and the mission behind it. Believe it or not, it all started in a small classroom at Milwaukee Area Technical College (MATC) with me the interior design instructor and Aga, the interior design student. From day one, we each made an impression on the other...we just didn't know it. Deeply rooted in that moment were our brands. I was the design-educated professional taking my career down a unique industry path, and Aga was the passionate student committed to her future and preparing for a successful career as an interior designer. The teacher-student, mentor-mentee relationship flourished with each class that brought us together. Our brands were evolving and our connection deepening.

The midpoint of our story was all about change. I stopped teaching to focus on my business and Aga was graduating, with her career just beginning. The strength of our personal brands was evident in this moment and our expanding networks were key to our success. For Aga, that translated into securing a full-time design position before she graduated. Meanwhile, I was leveraging my connections to grow my business.

We were both in a building mode when the economy hit rock bottom. Aga was one of many designers laid off at this time, and my design-focused client base had tough business decisions to make. Sometimes these career shocks can be just the push needed to head in a better direction. Aga turned this career challenge into an opportunity by starting her own business, and I looked for new ways to support my clients' marketing efforts.

Aga plunged head-first into the world of social media, and brought me along for the ride. The teacher-student, mentor-mentee tables started to turn as Aga introduced me to Twitter, Facebook, LinkedIn, etc. At networking events, we were both introducing each other to different connections. Our brands and our networking skills were not going unnoticed. Design professionals viewed us as unique businesswomen. Design instructors were asking us to speak to students about how to succeed post-graduation. We went from speaking separately to speaking together–and a partnership was born.

Class after class, school after school, career day after career day, we discussed issues related to personal branding, networking and strategic career development. We developed presentations for students and were also advising colleagues who were laid off or were looking for a change. Our brands were evolving again, but we were no longer just connectors. We were now resources for the industry.

Our challenge became: how do we communicate our message and help students and professionals in the course of an hour-long guest speaking opportunity or during a coffee meeting? It was on a ride to the University of Wisconsin-Stevens Point (my alma mater) that the idea of writing a book was born.

When people say that writing a book is a daunting task, they are not kidding. So much to say and how do we say it. It began with an outline and a proposal, then conversations with colleagues and industry leaders. There was writing, more writing and a lot of refining. The process took a great deal of time. In fact, it has been more than three years since we began this project–little did we know it would take us this long. Personal lives, heavy workloads and other unforeseen circumstances caused interruptions in our writing routine. When one of us was available and motivated to write, the other one was struggling with sleep deprivation due to a crazy work and life schedule. Still, we managed to push each other and make slow but steady progress. Was it a struggle? Yes. Was it fun? Yes. We learned so much about the process, the industry and each other.

Half-way through the project, we decided to expand the outline drastically. We now had ten chapters to write, not just the six that we started with. All these iterations made the process richer, and the book stronger and more insightful than we ever imagined.

As educated interior designers who have practiced within the profession and found success traveling unique career paths, we have walked in your shoes. Maybe not the same path, but we have contemplated similar subjects, like finding employment, switching careers or starting a business. We have helped other people tackle their design career obstacles. We have a focused approach to the subjects of personal branding, networking and strategic career development from an interior design perspective. We want to share this insight in order to help our fellow designers navigate the ups and downs of the industry and their personal careers.

So here it is–our book, *The Brand of You*. This isn't the end to our story. While we don't know what the future holds, we feel prepared to handle the twists and turns, because we have our brands to guide us. Our goal with this book is to guide others on a path to professional happiness. We hope it serves as a tool, a constant source of inspiration and information to help you grow and keep evolving. We will learn and find ways to continue to share our thoughts with you, so we can expand this book as the economy and industry challenge us all to evolve.

WHEN WE EMBARKED on this journey, we had lots of support from family, friends and the local design community. And it never changed. The further we got, the more love and enthusiasm we received. People would ask us all the time about the progress on the book. Strangers and good connections took interest in our project. We would not have finished without you.

We need to thank every professional who agreed to be interviewed and included in the book: Bill Lyons, Brian West, Robbyn Gabby, Jessica Mahnke, Ralph Ruder, Laura McDonald Stewart, Jean Chandler, Sandy Weber, Michelle Goertz and Stacy Garcia. We chose them for the impact they made, the unique stories they have to share and the passion they have for what they do. We wanted to show that success and happiness in the industry of interior design comes in many forms, and it is real.

Special thanks go to:

Our families (including our precious pups) and friends for ongoing support.

Sue Rebholz (Jenny's mom), Jodie Thill and Laura McDonald Stewart (cherished friends and valued colleagues) for feedback and red lines, which made the book that much better.

Phil Gerbyshak for sharing critical publishing knowledge, introducing contacts and keeping the excitement of our project alive. Jessie Dowd for rock star content editing, Wendi Van Eldik for beautiful book cover design and layout, Tricia Shay of ©Tricia Shay Photography for capturing our brands and the collaborative spirit of the book, Kira Henschel of HenschelHAUS Publishing for guidance and assistance with the publishing process (we would be so lost without you).The following venues, which provided a healthy dose of inspiration, caffeine and, of course, wine: The Ruby Tap, Colectivo Coffee, Stone Creek Coffee and Sven's Coffee.

CHAPTER 1

Introduction

A CAREER IS A journey, a commitment to traveling a path in search of professional fulfillment, happiness and success. No matter where you are on your journey, a bright-eyed student, an emerging professional or a seasoned designer, the foundation of your professional career is your education. With every year and each new employment opportunity, you build on that foundation, you learn more and gain more experience. You become an expert in your field. In addition to your education, we believe there is another important element required for your career journey–a personal brand. We see it as the vehicle that will help transport you from one destination to the next. We believe that your commitment to developing a personal brand will give you confidence, help you feel prepared and allow you to approach each opportunity and challenge along the way with optimism.

Personal branding is not a new topic. However, no matter the reference name ("You the Brand," "Brand You," etc.), the concept was, is and continues to be out of reach for some people. It is abstract and difficult to understand, and sometimes even uncomfortable. We have been talking to interior design students and seasoned design professionals about this for the last few years and continue to receive questions or have people reaching out for help, advice and words of encouragement. Why? Because some people simply don't know how to market themselves or where to even begin. Others understand the importance of branding, but aren't confident and underestimate the vast possibilities of their design education and experience.

In this book, our goal was to address content that is not typically covered in school and to help bridge the gap between the classroom and the professional world. And for those well beyond the classroom, we wanted to provide the support you need to take your career to the next level or make a change you have always wanted to make. We present the case that creativity and a design education offer a perfect foundation for success, but we fill most of the pages with such topics as self-analysis, diversification, messaging, networking, marketing, goal setting and strategic goal fulfillment. We offer personal stories, lessons learned and career advice in order to encourage and inspire you. We want to show you how other professionals have found success and happiness on their career journeys, so you can find your path to success and happiness, too.

Every chapter builds on the previous one, so we encourage you to read this book sequentially, but chapters can also be consumed individually, if you so desire. We wanted to write a book that can serve as a guide at any point in your career–a book that offers a quick reference, or one that can guide you through the branding process from start to finish. We even summarized each chapter and provided a list of additional resources to maximize your learning. Your experience with the book is entirely up to you. Our hope is that you will treat it as a career companion and return to it often.

We don't have all of the answers, but we do know that from time to time life will take you off guard. We hope this book will provide you with a strategic approach for taking control of your career path and handling the surprises along the way. We hope to open your eyes to greater possibilities. You have invested time and energy in a rewarding profession that offers many career options. We want to help you embrace and promote your unique brand as you enjoy the ride of your professional career with confidence, preparedness and optimism.

What This Book Is Not

If you are reading this book and expect us to give you the quick-fix solution to career success and prosperity, then stop right here. In fact, we want to set something straight. This book is not a textbook. It is not your standard guide for how-to-write-a-resume or how-to-build-a-portfolio. This book is not full of answers. This book is about the importance of developing a personal brand to carry you through your career journey. In fact, it is full of questions. It is a guide for preparing, positioning and tackling the career challenges ahead.

The Purpose

Our stories and our commitment to find happiness in our own careers have turned into a purposeful passion to teach others how to see themselves as unique brands. We are certainly not experts. We are life-long students. As we grow and learn, we want to share the knowledge we have gained and vice versa. We do appreciate and value every connection we made while writing this book, and look forward to new connections and opportunities this book may bring.

No matter where you are in your journey, we want to help. Whether you have a clear understanding of who you are or are completely confused and afraid, we are here to help you.

We want you to be a healthy, happy, successful professional. So many hours of our lives are spent working. We want you to find enjoyment in what you do and how you do it.

Our brands have served us well so far, and we believe yours will too. Are you ready to begin a life-long career journey with your brand in focus? Always changing, never completely done, a personal brand is like a baby–it's your blood and your soul; it requires your full attention and commitment. And, in the end, it makes you eternally proud and happy.

Think About. . .

What is your story?

Where are you in your career journey?

Are you ready to embrace change?

Are you ready to take control of your career?

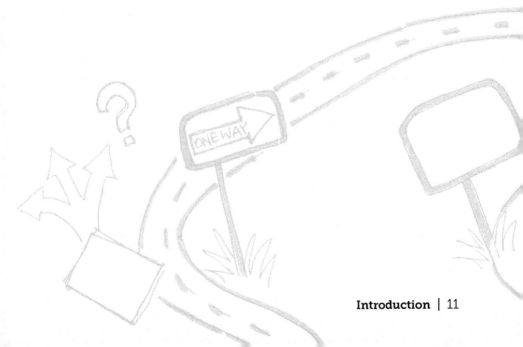

CHAPTER 2

The Fuel and the Factors

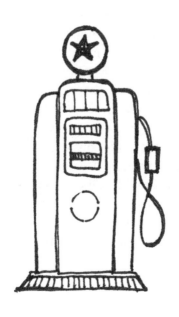

CONGRATULATIONS ON CHOOSING interior design as your career path. It's a bold and cheer-worthy move. Huurraayy! A career in interior design is exciting. No two days are the same, which is a reason in itself to love or hate this profession. Interior design is a career, not just a job. Interior designers don't just show up, do their work and leave. We live and breathe design. We take inspiration from the world around us. In traveling, dining out or strolling around town, life inspires us, places inspire us and people inspire us. The smallest detail can provoke an idea, generate a solution and bring us back into the game. We are constantly "on," and we love it.

There is a fuel to this fire in our bellies, and it is this fuel that will help you take your career to the next level. Creativity, passion and the willingness to embrace change will allow you to adapt and succeed no matter what the industry and economy throw your way.

Creativity

There are many definitions to creativity, but when you study the word itself, two distinct words emerge: create and activity. And as such, it promotes innovation, progress and growth. It is a unique skill; or better yet, creativity is irreplaceable. In a constantly evolving world, creativity is considered one of the most critical skills. Whether it's interior design, architecture, photography or painting, creatives have this in common—we look at the problem at hand and develop ideas, concepts and solutions that fix it. We don't just create pretty solutions; we create solutions that work.

How can creativity save the day and set you apart from others? At work, it's not all smooth-sailing. Problems arise all the time, and most often unexpectedly. How would you react in that circumstance? Would you try to understand the issue, remember the goal and quickly come up with a viable solution to present to your boss or client? Or would you react emotionally (freak out), allowing the moment to influence your judgment, throwing your hands in the air and shouting "What now!?"

Can you see the difference? Can you guess which individual employers and clients would rather have on their team? Unless it's a drama queen contest, we're assuming you agree that the first candidate–the one who kept her cool and thought rationally and critically about the issue–prevailed.

Creative people who succeed in the real world are the ones who apply their design education. This education serves as a foundation– it provides you with a process-oriented way of thinking that is extremely valuable to a variety of employers and beneficial to clients. This process allows you to dissect all types of challenges. You know how to research and brainstorm to generate a variety of solutions, some typical and others that are totally out-of-the-box. This is the value of your creativity. This is what makes you an asset.

Creatives think differently and bring a unique perspective to the table. Do you find yourself questioning the normal and challenging the status quo? We do. When something is not going right, do you look for ways to improve processes or develop new products? We do (that's why we wrote this book). Today's world needs creative problem-solvers; it needs critical thinkers, not status-quo defenders; leaders, not followers. Today's world needs you.

Passion

An intensity, a drive, a devotion, a deep interest–your passion for interior design is an essential ingredient in the fuel that keeps you going. Think about it: would you really have completed design school without it? Isn't it this passion that somehow kept you going? Isn't it your passion for design that brought you to where you are today? You most likely have annoyed a friend or two with your need to touch and feel a finish or a fabric. You surely have received awkward looks when you flipped that chair upside down just to see who made it. This passion has kept you up late at night looking at a lighting catalog, searching online for the perfect accessory or reading every design magazine you can get your hands on.

Chances are your decision to become a professional interior designer wasn't mathematical, but rather emotional. You want to love what you do, feel passionate about going to work every day. Money is oftentimes secondary. With a median hourly rate of $22.89 and a median yearly salary of $47,600, designers make a good living, but only a lucky few become millionaires.[1]

A career in interior design is not easy. We all have stories to share about our highs and lows. When projects derail, clients become difficult to deal with or budgets get cut, something keeps us going—and that something is passion. When you are laid off from your job (as we both were, though at different times) or just feel the need for a change, your passion for design pushes you. Your passion will fuel you throughout this book. It is what you need to make changes in your career path and your life. It is what you look to for comfort and reassurance that you are doing the right thing.

It may not be a straight path. In fact, careers in interior design are typically everything but linear. It's the most exciting, and equally the most nerve-wracking, part about it. Not everyone sees the possibilities or takes advantage of them. We know you can. Equipped with a great education, creativity and passion, you can truly do anything.

Change

Change is a fact of life. Change, self-imposed or totally unexpected, is a factor that will impact your career journey. In a world where companies and products launch and fold again in the blink of an eye, one must realize the potential of change, the value in the constant improvement of a process and the idea that things are never complete, never perfect. And that's okay.

Along with change comes the inevitable–failure. If it's not what you thought it would be, is that an automatic failure? You can't think like that. In fact, if you failed at reaching a goal, you've actually done more than most people. You have given it a try. Do you remember when you were learning to ride a bicycle? Did you hop on and take off on the first try? Or did you fall a few times only to get right back up and try again? Failure is a step in the process of reaching the destination. You may need to re-evaluate things, revise the path and alter the goal. What's the worst that could happen? Success?

Sometimes you choose to make a change. However, there will be other times where that change is imposed upon you. We challenge you to embrace these sudden, unexpected and even frightening moments as an opportunity for reinvention. Don't worry. It is okay to take a moment to be shocked, hurt, sad, angry, etc. We are all human, so give yourself permission to pout for a day. But don't waste too much time sulking. Instead, jump back on your feet–your career bike, so to speak–and prepare for your reinvention.

As designers, aren't we asking people to embrace change all the time? We alter their "live, work, play" environments to address problems at hand. Sometimes our design solutions include minor changes. Other times, we recommend full-fledged demolition and reconstruction to make things better. If we want others to change, shouldn't we be willing to change, too? As designers, don't we fundamentally believe change is good? We do, and we are asking you to apply that belief to your own career, whether it is a small change or a complete career overhaul. We understand that a new direction, position or course of action is scary–the uncertainty is sometimes paralyzing, but it is normal. Embrace that fear. Use it as your fuel.

The Economy and the State of the Industry

You are creative, passionate and willing to embrace change. You are ready to take on the world! What does the world have in store for you? The economy and the state of the industry are factors that will impact your career journey. These are elements that are out of your control, yet how you monitor the patterns of these current events and anticipate the effect they will have on your business or employment will be crucial to your success.

The economy has a dramatic effect on the design profession. Many interior designers can share stories (our own stories, for example) of how the economy and job market impacted their career choices from one decade to the next. The financial crisis of 2008-2009 had a profound impact industry-wide on interior designers, architects and construction workers. Job security? Ha! What is that? Entry-level, mid-level and senior designers, even executives in firms, were all vulnerable. Each day, another talented designer would be jobless. The total number of practicing interior designers has dramatically declined since its peak prior to the recession, from 72,082 in 2007 to 56,766 in 2013.[2] Classrooms full of interior design students worried about what would happen after graduation. The lack of confidence in the profession could be seen in the number of graduates with bachelor's degrees, as it dropped between 2008 and 2009 from 4,430 to 4,234.[3]

History tends to repeat itself, and every generation most likely will experience what life is like before, during and after an economic crisis. The good news is that after a recession, there tends to be a period of growth and expansion. The current state of the interior design industry is optimistic. The U.S. Bureau of Labor Statistics identifies interior design as a growing industry, at an average rate of 13 percent.[4] According to the ASID industry research report, the industry has fully recovered to pre-recession levels, with 60,824 employed interior designers and 13,257 design firms.[5]

When you look closely at the many different positions interior designers hold, an even more positive picture can be painted. The statistics we mentioned above only recognize the traditional definition of an interior designer. Positions such as manufacturer's representatives and account executives, consultants and freelancers, facilities designers, project managers and other non-standard job titles are not part of this traditional definition, but are viable career paths. This makes the future outlook for design-related opportunities even better.

Just remember, life is a roller coaster ride full of ups and downs, as well as twists and turns. Just when you think you are safe, something happens to prove the opposite to be true. Pay attention to more than your client's challenges. Pay attention to what is going on at your company. As an employee, do you know what it takes to keep the business profitable? If you are self-employed, are you spending as much time promoting your business as you are working on your client projects? Just because you have enough work today doesn't mean you will tomorrow. You have to continuously market your services to maintain a steady flow of work. Are you paying attention to the state of the client's company? What if they put a project on hold because they suddenly can't afford you or reduce the amount of the retainer you count on to pay your bills? Don't let the economy surprise you.

All About You

As you make career decisions, it is important to be true to yourself. People in your life will always have opinions. Choosing a career based on a push or someone else's hunch, and not your own inner voice or passion, is trouble waiting to happen. You don't want to make a change because someone told you to or miss an opportunity because of his or her opinion. Your inner voice and gut feelings need to guide you.

In some cases, money will be a distraction in the decision-making process. Be careful of this temptation. Don't make any decisions based solely on money. If the money sounds too good to be true, then it just might be. If the money sounds great, but your gut is nervous about other factors, trust your gut. There may be times in your life when the need for money may require a tough decision. If you need to make that choice, then have a plan for how you are going to get yourself back on track to where your passion lies. Ultimately, we have found that following your passion will lead you in a better direction and will get you financially where you want to be.

A career in interior design is a long-term commitment. Who in their right mind would choose a career path that is this demanding, this unknown and this challenging? Only design nuts like us! It's not insanity, just pure joy and a whole-hearted passion that are to blame. Be true to yourself and stick to what you love.

A career in interior design is not easy, so it is the fuel that will keep you going even when you question what you are doing with your life. Believe us, at some point it will become clear. Your creativity, passion and willingness to embrace change will help you tackle any challenges that the state of the industry and economy throw your way. And your fuel will be critical as you develop the most important tool to help you face career obstacles–*The Brand of You*.

Think About. . .

Your creativity is an asset.

Your passion will carry you through this process.

Change will happen. You can equip yourself to better handle it.

Be aware of the world around you. Watch for industry and economic patterns.

Don't choose a path because you are told to—make sure it is the right choice for you.

Your career journey will go in many directions. Each step—the good, the bad, the successes and failures—is building toward something greater. The place you are meant to be.

Explore

On creativity, passion and change:
1. *Linchpin* by Seth Godin
2. *A Whole New Mind* by Daniel Pink
3. *Who Moved My Cheese?* by Spencer Johnson

On the practice of interior design:
1. *Professional Practice for Interior Designers* by Christine M. Piotrowski
2. *The Interior Design Business Handbook* by Mary V. Knackstedt
3. *Interior Design in Practice: Case Studies of Successful Business Models* by Terri Maurer and Katie Weeks

On the state of the economy and the interior design industry:
1. *Interior Design 2015/2016 Outlook and State of the Industry* by ASID
2. *Occupational Outlook Handbook* by United States Department of Labor, Bureau of Labor Statistics
3. *ADP Employment Reports* by ADP Research Institute®

CHAPTER 3

The Brand of You

I N A WORLD over-saturated with content, how do people ensure their message is seen and heard? And for that matter, what is your message? And why? What is your brand? How do you define and develop a professional identity that will help clearly state who you are, help you reach your career goals and be your lifeline whenever your career path changes course? Start thinking about yourself in terms of *The Brand of You.*

What Is a Brand?

A brand is a connection, a relationship and a promise. It is not a logo, a mark or a stamp. You may have the most eye-catching logo and business card on the planet, but if you have not conveyed what you stand for and have not created a relationship with your audience or network, it won't get you far. Your logo can change or be forgotten, and your business card can end up buried under hundreds of new ones. It's the *why*, not the *what* that matters most.

A Brand Is a Promise

Apple's unspoken promise is to amaze and give its customers something they never even thought they needed. Nike's promise is one of product quality and commitment to an advanced athletic solution. Your dentist's promise is to provide exceptional preventive care and make you feel at ease. What's your promise?

As a student of interior design, your promise should be to attend classes, learn as much as you can and turn your homework in on time. If you are beyond college, working for a firm or for yourself, showing up is still important, as is meeting deadlines. It is hard to make a good impression on your boss or a client if you consistently fail to make it to the office, a meeting or complete assignments on time.

Seems pretty simple to us–do what you say you will. But believe it or not, a surprising number of people fail to fulfill even such easy requirements. What does that say about them? What if your dentist showed up late to every appointment and only examined half of your teeth? Don't develop bad habits. If you make a promise, keep it.

Big Brands That Do It Right

Apple consistently delivers unique electronic solutions to its users, who have been taught to expect a lot. With every new product introduction, Apple raises the bar even higher. The iPod was revolutionary for its time–so were the iPhone, the iPad and whatever comes next. But Apple's branding effort doesn't end there. It is apparent in its digital marketing, as well as in their retail design. Speaking of innovation, their concept of an on-site help desk, called the Genius Bar, was, well, genius. If you engage with your customers and make them feel like a part of the solution, you show them you care. They will be more likely to return for more "genius" advice in the future.

Nike, on the other hand, has positioned itself as a leader in athletic footwear and garments. The Nike "swoosh" is widely known and recognizable, but it's doubtful that customers buy Nike purely for its logo. There is more behind that graphic. The brand is quality, commitment and passion. The design of their stores, as often as it is updated, reflects the same values. You know where you are when you step inside a Nike store.

Brand Loyalty and Authenticity

Have you ever been in a Disney store, on a Disney cruise or to Disneyland? Now that's who we consider a master of branding. Disney was founded in 1923, so it has been refining its brand for nearly a century. We believe that we can all learn a lot from Disney's way of building life-long relationships with its customers. That's what it is good at. We don't buy into a Disney story solely for the logo or Mickey Mouse (although we all love him). Can you confirm that your last experience with Disney was truly wonderful and authentic? Did it make you feel special? Did Disney create a level of trust that will keep you coming back and spreading the positive feedback about your experience? Yes, yes and yes. That's the type of response you want to create with *The Brand of You*–the more personal and genuine, the better.

Brand Perception

It matters what people think and say about a brand. A branding campaign is only successful if it touches the heart of the consumer, makes a memorable impact and causes an emotional reaction. In other words, it's not what you say your brand is–it's what others perceive that matters most. It's one thing to say that you create magic (such as our example of Disney). But it's not until a consumer has a magical experience at a Disney store or in a Disney park, that his brand perception is created (and it's a good one).

Why Do You Need a Brand?

You've heard the saying, "The only constant is change." Well, it applies directly to the interior design industry. When you started your career, were jobs plentiful or scarce? Today, the industry is growing, but no one knows for sure what the future will bring. In the past, employment made people believe in job security and they often stayed employed by one company for many years or their entire professional career. People identified themselves with the company they worked for. Look no further than the economic crisis of 2008, when hundreds of experienced professionals lost their positions. They had worked for a firm so long that they felt lost without the company's brand behind them.

We believe having a consistent *Brand of You* is the new way to achieve a sense of security. Don't let your place of employment define you. Learn what you can, be committed and be honest about your long-term goals, but at the same time, never lose sight of who you are and what you bring to the table. If you accept an amazing offer with the firm of your dreams, think of yourself as a designer on a semi-permanent contract. You are lending your skills, your knowledge and your brand to the firm that hired you. If something goes wrong, you can walk away with your head up and the same clear vision you started with. *The Brand of You* stays with you forever; employment is temporary.

Defining *The Brand of You*

We hope that it now makes sense, why committing time to understanding and developing *The Brand of You* is critical to your career's viability and, more so, success. Now, let's look at how to actually build one.

The idea of a person being a brand is not new. It's been written and talked about before. Tom Peters explained the concept in an article for *Fast Company* Magazine in 1997:

> *"Regardless of age, regardless of position, regardless of the business we happen to be in, all of us need to understand the importance of branding. We are CEOs of our own companies: Me Inc. To be in business today, our most important job is to be head marketer for the brand called You."* [6]

The Brand of You is your promise to the world. It communicates your core values, your competencies, your unique personality, your life experiences and even your faults. *The Brand of You* is what you will stand up for and what you will stand behind. At the end of the day, it is what you are left with. Now is the time to really think about your brand and the message you are conveying to those around you. When you go to bed at night, can you fall asleep knowing you have been the best you that you can be today?

The Strategy Behind *The Brand of You*

Companies of every size go through a similar evaluation process in order to create a strategic marketing and business plan, so you can create one, too. Here are the big questions you should ask yourself:

- *Who am I?*
- *What is my situation?*
- *What are my goals and objectives?*

Who Are You?

We want you to really think about yourself. What are your strengths, what work ethic are you bringing to the workplace and what do you really stand for? We encourage you to spend some time conducting a self-analysis. There are many self-help resources out there to assist you as you figure out who you are. We found *Now, Discover Your Strengths* by Marcus Buckingham and Donald O. Clifton to be a comprehensive source, but there are many others.

Your Strengths And Weaknesses

This whole process starts with you and your ability to recognize your strengths and weaknesses. This is the essence of you, the details and characteristics that create *The Brand of You*. According to Buckingham and Clifton:

> *"Your talents, your strongest synaptic connections, are the most important raw material for strength building. Identify your most powerful talents, hone them with skills and knowledge, and you will be well on your way to living the strong life."* [7]

The key is to focus on the strengths. The world's best managers know this and you should too– *"Each person's greatest room for growth is in the area of his or her greatest strengths."* [8] So again, look within yourself. Identify your natural and unique talents, pinpoint your greatest strengths, and focus on those.

Consider the following skills–are they strengths, weaknesses or something in between?

- Proficiency/deficiency in architectural software (AutoCAD, Revit, Sketchup)
- Proficiency/deficiency in graphic software (Photoshop, Publisher)
- Oral communication or presentation
- Written communication
- Foreign languages
- Graphic design
- Photography

- Financial acumen and budget management
- Inventory and logistics
- Scheduling
- Time management
- Attention to detail
- Organization
- Selling ability
- Listening
- Team building and participation
- Reliability and trustworthiness
- Accountability
- Introverted/extroverted personality
- One-on-one interactions
- Detail-orientation
- Strategic thinking
- Follow through
- *Add more to your list*

What are you learning about yourself? Are you seeing ways you can differentiate yourself from the competition?

Your Interests

Besides design, what other areas of interest are you passionate about? They may or may not be related to your education and current employment. As you start to define *The Brand of You*, these may find a more prominent place. Connections between your education, experiences and hobbies can often lead your career in new, interesting and, ultimately, fulfilling directions. Can you imagine your passion for baking leading you to opening your own bakery? And you, of course, have the skills necessary to design the retail space. Or you take your pet to an obedience school, the owner of which is expanding her business and hires you to do the build-out. Who knows? You may like it so much that pet-focused design becomes your specialty.

What are you into? What are your hobbies?

- Health/fitness
- Sustainability
- Photography
- Children
- Helping others
- Fashion
- Cooking or baking
- Art (paintings, sculpture, etc.)
- Traveling
- Foreign languages
- Theater
- Dance
- Sports
- Beer
- Wine
- Pets

- Jewelry
- Scrapbooking
- Politics
- Weddings
- Gardening
- Writing
- *Add more to your list*

Your Credentials

You may choose to pursue (or perhaps you already have) certain industry credentials to align your strengths and areas of interest, and position yourself for success within the industry. Obtaining specific credentials may be a goal for your own self-fulfillment and/or a strategic decision for building your brand and differentiating you from the competition.

One of the most important credentials an interior designer can obtain is the National Council for Interior Design Qualification (NCIDQ). It is an exam that tests your broad knowledge of both the fundamental theory and the practical knowledge of the profession. This certification acknowledges that you are "a professional with proven knowledge, experience and proficiency in the interior design principles of protecting the public health, safety and welfare."[9] In order to qualify to sit for the exam, a candidate must meet the minimum education and certain amount hours of field experience. However, NCIDQ is now allowing graduates of Interior Design from a Council for Interior Design Association (CIDA) accredited school to take one of three parts at the start of their careers (whether you are employed or not). Those who opt to take the exam early demonstrate their commitment to their careers. Taking and successfully passing the first part could be perceived as a competitive advantage in the search for employment.

Other design-related credentials worth investigating include:

- Leadership in Energy and Environmental Design (LEED)
- American Academy of Healthcare Interior Designer (AAHID)
- Certified Aging in Place Specialist (CAPS)
- Certified Facility Manager (CFM)
- Evidence-based Design Accreditation and Certification (EDAC)
- Certified Lighting Consultant (CLC)
- Lighting Certification (LC) by National Council for Qualifications for the Lighting Professions
- Associate Kitchen and Bath Designer (AKBD)
- Certified Kitchen Designer (CKD)
- Certified Bath Designer (CBD)
- Certified Master Kitchen and Bath Designer (CMKBD)
- Master's Degree in a specific subject: Interior Design, Education

Look into the credentialing requirements. Some of them can be obtained fairly quickly; others will need time to be executed. Along the way, you may also discover that you have a strong interest in a related field, like real estate, landscape design or architecture. An interior design degree is a great springboard for exploring a variety of interests. It is a solid educational foundation to build on. Acquiring credentials can help validate the choices you make and demonstrate your commitment to professional success. However, be careful of acquiring a list of credentials just to have a long list of letters after your name. It takes a lot of work, money and ongoing education to maintain credentials from year to year, so choose wisely.

Your Code

We all have a sense of right and wrong. This guides our decision-making both personally and professionally. You may find yourself thinking about new opportunities because your current employer uses business practices that conflict with your code of ethics (race, religion, politics, sexual orientation, leadership styles, etc.). What are your values and how important is it for them to be in line with your employer and your co-workers?

Take some time to think about what is important to you and your value system. Write down your non-negotiable code of ethics.

Your Supportive Environment

To be a peak performer, what working conditions do you need? There are a variety of factors to consider (size of the company, management style, the physical environment, specific working conditions, etc.).

What type of environment do you excel in?

- A large corporate environment with multiple offices
- An international company
- A medium-sized company
- A small company
- A family-owned business
- A home office
- A sales-driven organization
- A retail environment
- A big city

- A rural town
- East Coast, West Coast, Midwest, the South, Southwest, etc.
- A position that requires a lot of travel
- A position that requires public speaking and presentation skills
- A company where you are assigned a mentor/mentee
- An energetic, active environment with a lot of teamwork
- A quiet office setting with mostly individual work assignments
- A funky office design
- A conservative office setting
- A big-decision-making hierarchy
- One boss to answer to
- Being your own boss
- An environment where you work on a few big projects over the course of a few years
- A setting where you do a lot of small projects with quick turnaround deadlines
- A company where you make a set salary
- A commission-based salary
- A base with opportunities for commission and bonus payments
- A comprehensive benefits package
- Incentives for hard work
- High expectations
- Vacation/personal time is a priority
- A company that has flex-time
- A company that understands family comes first

- Part-time work

- Full-time work

- Punch a clock

- Work, work, work...you love to work

As you can see, there are many factors to consider when determining what a supportive work environment means to you. You may not know until you try it. You might think a commission-based salary is not for you, only to learn that money motivates you to do your best work. You may think a family-owned business sounds perfect until you learn more about the family than you ever wanted to know.

Your preferences may change as your personal life changes over the years. You may be ready to work, work, work and travel all the time in your twenties, but want a part-time situation that allows you to stay home and raise a family later on. As life circumstances require, you may need to take a position you know isn't the perfect fit. It is okay to change your mind. In fact, this process of self-analysis is something you should do often. It's sort of like your life insurance policy. With every major change in your life, you should review it and adjust as necessary.

What Is Your Situation?

Now that you are figuring out who you are and what *The Brand of You* really stands for, you need to establish where you want to go. But, in order to decide where you want to go, you need to truly reflect on where you have been and where you are right now. This is textbook marketing strategy: the situation analysis. Take the time to reflect and be honest with yourself. Think about the following questions, take some notes or start a journal so you have this information handy as you establish *The Brand of You*. It will also allow you to come back to this again if you decide it is time for another change.

What do you like and dislike about your current situation?

From the location and type of work setting to the people you work with and your job responsibilities, what do you like and what drives you crazy?

What would make you happy?

If money were not a factor, what would you be doing? Most likely, if you are going through this process, you are unhappy in your current situation. The hard part is figuring out what you think will make you happy. Some people may clearly know the answer to this, while others may soul-search for years. You could discover that what you think will make you happy only leads you back through this process again. No worries: Remember trial and error is part of this process.

What is your budget?

Everyone has budget limitations, but no matter how high or low that number is, you can accomplish your goals. Maybe you want to move and not having a job for a few months is not an option. Perhaps part of your goal is gaining further education, but you can't afford to enroll in a master's program. Or you need to invest in new technology or a new website to better promote *The Brand of You*. What can your budget handle? Don't forget to account for the value of your time and energy. How much blood, sweat, tears, hours, days or years are you willing to invest?

Do you have a timeline in mind?

Do you have a time limit for accomplishing your goals? While this process takes time, life or your lack of patience may impose some time restrictions on your goals. Whether you need to find a job in a new city because your significant other is relocating for business, you just graduated and need to support yourself, your current job is impacting your health or you were just laid off–the element of time may impact the decisions you make. The effect of this clock may mean you need a few extra steps in between to finally get you where you really wanted to go in the first place. You may have all the time in the world. If your current job is okay, you can stick it out until you can make the perfect next move.

Just remember to stay on top of the state of the economy and industry so that you are not living with a false sense of comfort. This means staying on top of the state of the company, too. Just because the world outside is looking good doesn't mean your position at a specific company is secure. It's always better to make a move when you don't have to, when it's least expected by others, but meticulously planned and backed by you.

Who are you competing against? What makes you different?

In business and in life, you have to know who or what you are competing against. You have spent a fair amount of time outlining elements of *The Brand of You*. What if your strengths and weaknesses are the same as someone else? How can you differentiate yourself from the rest? These differences are the essence of *The Brand of You*. Think about the opportunity you are pursuing and who you are competing against. What attributes and differentiators might they be bringing to the table? If you are all recent graduates or mid-level designers or seasoned professionals applying for the same opening, what sets you apart? What is the job description and how can you position yourself to be at the top of the list? Similarly, when you are interviewing for a project, which other firms have been invited to present? What do they offer that you or your firm doesn't? What differentiators will raise your firm to the top of the list?

This is where a combination of your skills, expertise and interests starts to lay the groundwork for a truly unique brand. Consider the following example:

As you interview for a design position, you show your design portfolio and outline your experience. During the presentation, you express your ability to take quality project photos. All of a sudden, a potential employer sees a way to improve the company's image library without increasing its budget for professional photography. Your experience with specific graphic and design software and ability to write allows you to support the marketing team, too. The employer sees the value in the unique skills you present and hires you on the spot.

But, perhaps you are more interested in a consulting role and want to build a business based on your unique proposition. You realize that your diverse skills hold a lot of value. During a meeting with the same organization, you pitch your new company and its consulting services that include interior photography and proposal writing. The same prospect may be open to hiring a project-based consultant like you rather than filling a full-time position.

As an employee or a consultant, how can you present value and use *The Brand of You* to stand out?

What is the state of the economy?

It is important to understand what is going on in the world around you. But where does one go to find these clues? Unfortunately, there is not one place. Watch and read news stories and make mental notes of important happenings. But don't limit yourself to the local news. In fact, make time to tune into international channels, such as the British Broadcasting Corporation (BBC), or national television or radio stations like National Public Radio (NPR). Travel and talk to people to learn their point of view. Paying attention to the housing market, gas prices and other economic factors that will help you stay ahead in the game of life as much as possible. If you are good at it, you may see signs of staff cuts ahead, so you can start looking for a new opportunity before you wake up without a job.

What is the state of the industry?

Be aware of how the economy is specifically impacting the architecture, design and construction world. If you are focused on being a hospitality designer, but the hotel market is collapsing, that might change your focus. If there is going to be a spike in retail design, you may decide to pick up some additional skills to make you a better fit for that market. Attend industry events, read design publications, review the real estate section of the local newspaper. It may be a little dry, but we even indulge in a monthly publication titled, *ADP National Employment Report.* It shows a short-term employment change in the nonfarm, private sector from real data derived from more than 24 million U.S. workers. It's a fascinating read. Find sources that fascinate you and keep you abreast. Analyze and synthesize the information and draw your own conclusions.

What Are Your Goals and Objectives?

Your Goals

A key part of developing your strategic plan is identifying your goals. What do you want? In the big picture, where do you see yourself? A goal is an overarching vision. It can be broad, abstract and intangible. Based on our encounters with design students and professionals over the years (and the numerous discussions, coffee meetings and emails), the overarching goals interior designers set for themselves are:

- Find employment
- Switch a career path
- Start a business

Your Objectives

If a goal is broad and abstract, an objective ought to be narrow, precise and tangible. An objective is a measurable, concrete aim toward reaching your goal. The "object" part of the word narrows down the goal to a single focus and calls for a quantitative approach. Learning a foreign language could be your goal. But getting to a conversational level of Spanish in three months is a definite objective. How you get there is a matter of identifying the appropriate tactics.

Our professional goal is to empower interior designers to build successful careers. That's a pretty broad goal. Providing personal branding and career development advice that can reach hundreds, hopefully thousands, simultaneously is an objective. This book becomes a tactic. It is a vehicle, which helps us reach many more professionals than we can physically meet in the course of a day, thus empowering them to build successful careers. Writing the book is in line with our overall objective and the goal. It is a means for consolidating and organizing the information, knowledge and experiences we want to share.

What are your objectives? If finding employment is your goal, a narrower focus could be your objective. Where do you want to work, what city, what firm, what type of position, by when? Your objective should be tangible and focused. For example: "I want to obtain full-time employment with a commercial furniture dealership where I can utilize my excellent interpersonal skills and ability to sell." The objective is built based on your answers to the previous sections of the self-analysis (who you are and what is your situation). If you skipped one or both of those parts, you may want to go back and really dive in.

Later in the book, we will address specific tactics to help you fulfill your objective and reach your goal. Having an overarching goal allows you the freedom to change directions along your career path. As long as you know where you are going and why you do what you do, things will start making more sense. Don't just take it from us. The next few chapters will showcase stories of many designers and their winding paths to success. We want you to see that there is not one interior design mold for everyone to fit and not one path to take. These professionals have created their own brands and found different positions to support their success and happiness over the years. You can, too!

Think About. . .

A brand is a connection, a relationship and a promise.
Take some time. Think about yourself.

- Who are you?
- What is your situation?
- What are your goals and objectives?

What type of work makes you happy?

If money weren't a concern, what would you be doing?

Explore

On self-discovery:
1. *Now, Discover Your Strengths* by Marcus Buckingham and Donald O. Cliffton
2. *StrengthsFinder 2.0* by Tom Rath
3. *What Color Is Your Parachute* by Richard N. Bolles
4. *Start With Why* by Simon Sinek

A re you overwhelmed yet? All of this talk about the future and thinking strategically can be exciting, but stressful. For some of you, this may be new, while others have heard it before, but never really committed to developing a strategy. Our knowledge has been built over the years, and we want you to understand that we have been in your shoes. We continue to evaluate ourselves, re-assess our goals and change direction as necessary. You are not alone.

Give your brain a rest for a minute. Stop thinking about all that you have to do and instead learn from our stories and the stories of other design professionals who have inspired us along the way. We use career maps to illustrate the twists and turns of everyone's career journey. These drawings communicate personal details (key moments, influential people, reasons behind career decisions, etc.) that would not be visible in a traditional resume format. The professionals we will be highlighting will resurface throughout the book to offer additional comments and advice. We hope these stories will inspire and show you that there is a world of possibilities when you start thinking strategically about your career journey and *The Brand of You*.

CHAPTER 4

Jenny's Career Journey

Education

FROM THE BEGINNING, I knew what I wanted...or so I thought. I was very specific when selecting a college–I wanted a school that offered both interior design and communications majors. With early admissions to the University of Wisconsin-Stevens Point, I was on my way. People seemed confused by my combination of majors, but it was always clear to me and became evident to my fellow design students when it was time to give a presentation. I loved school. I loved design. My academic achievements and portfolio proved I was pretty good, but as graduation grew near, I already was fairly confident I would not spend the rest of my life as a designer. I was smart enough to realize that I didn't know enough about design. I felt it was necessary to put my education to the test and gain some practical design experience.

Experience

Throughout school, internships and the pursuit of my first design position, I focused on commercial design. I was enamored with large corporate office spaces, retail environments and hospitality design. My first position actually evolved from pure networking, although I didn't realize the power of networking at the time. I had heard a woman speak at Career Day during college about her job at a design-build furniture dealership. I spoke to her after the session, followed up with her and secured an internship with the company the summer before my final year in school. The success of that internship and maintaining communications with key contacts at the company led to the first step in my career journey.

I was ambitious from day one, wondering when I would have my own clients. Having great mentors helps you keep things in perspective. The team at that first company provided me with a solid foundation and gave me the skills I needed to support my inner drive. Part of that drive included assisting with marketing and other communications tasks, which the company willingly accepted. I was gaining experience in design and marketing, just because I was an overachiever. That would pay off far more than I knew at the time.

While I was enjoying my role with this company, I was personally restless. Due to time spent abroad and an initial effort to find a job out of state, I had a deep need to travel, explore different cities and experience new cultures. I knew that if I didn't leave the Milwaukee area then, I never would. Furthermore, as a designer, I was really interested in hospitality work and needed to go to a market that offered more of those opportunities. Through a college friend I had a connection to a designer in Phoenix. After a few phone calls and a copy of the *Business Journal's* top Phoenix-area architectural firms, I created a target list of job prospects.

Being the mid- to late-90s, there weren't websites to review or emails to send. This was about old-fashioned cover letters, resumes and follow-up all summer long, until I had a "vacation" planned. Walking the line between annoying and persistent, I continued to follow up until I had a yes or a no. I confirmed one interview, then two... and by the time I was lugging my huge portfolio case onto the plane, I had nine interviews set up for one week. After nine interviews and two follow-up interviews in the crazy Phoenix heat, I returned home on a Sunday. I received a job offer that Monday, accepted it Tuesday, resigned Wednesday and two weeks later, I was in my car moving to Arizona. Sometimes you just need to take a leap of faith.

I continued to gain valuable design experience in Arizona with two different firms over the next three-and-a-half years, with a specific focus in hospitality design. With each firm, I once again offered to support writing and marketing efforts, which continued to grow my resume in multiple directions. The move to Phoenix and the job changes I made there were how the power of networking and personal branding became clear to me. After my move, and sending thank-you notes to everyone I interviewed with, I heard that people were asking about me. I had created a reputation for myself in a city where I hardly knew anyone. As I looked to make job changes, relationships I developed with specific manufacturers' reps helped me to secure great opportunities throughout my career journey.

These relationships became even more important as I started to feel restless as a designer. I was working on amazing hospitality projects under the guidance of some truly talented professionals. They were ready to take me under their wings and make me a great designer, but my heart wasn't in it. The small amount of time I spent writing or working on a marketing project was providing the greatest amount of job satisfaction. Now what? What do I want to be when I grow up?

NEVER SAY NEVER

I always tell people to remain open to the possibilities, which is what led me back to Wisconsin. At that time, I thought I would never move back—but here I am still. That is why I now say, "Never say never." Life is full of surprises. If you remain open to new things and face the unknown with a positive attitude, you just might be presented with an incredible opportunity that you never expected.

My network in Arizona connected me with all types of people who were filling my head with so many ideas and suggestions (be an art teacher, go into advertising, etc.). Then one person called my attention to working in marketing for an architectural firm. As usual, things happen for a reason, and personal and professional life moments collided to lead me down a new path. My grandfather passed away and my first niece was born—I started to think about moving closer to home. So, I called one of my best friends, Suzanne Koch (the woman I heard speak on Career Day). I told her I was looking for something in marketing in Chicago or Milwaukee. The company she was working for at the time was looking for someone to fill that position. Several interviews and a long car ride later, I was back in Milwaukee. I left Arizona and life as a designer behind. I was now the marketing manager at a design-build furniture dealership.

I learned so much and grew in so many ways professionally in that marketing position, but at the heart of the success was the foundation I had built–the design education and experience. After three years and the recession post-9/11, I was feeling restless in the corporate world and the company could no longer support my position. Once again, I took a leap in a direction I never had imagined for myself, and I decided to start my own business. Many companies had been laying off marketing positions, but they still had work to be done. I believed there was a niche I could fill with minimal competition. I needed to work outside of the 9-to-5 structured corporate environment. I needed a change and starting my own business seemed like the only option.

Entrepreneurship

While I am not the poster child for how to properly start a business, I am the kind of person who just needs to jump in and do it. This is when my wide and diverse network came into play and rapidly expanded. I called everyone I knew, telling them what I was going to do. I created a support network for setting up my business properly. I moved in with my grandmother to help make things possible financially. I hit the ground running.

The business was focused on writing and marketing. I wrote for several design publications and began to do small marketing and PR projects for companies. I named the business Jenny S. Rebholz LLC. Due to the writing I was doing, my name was my byline and an easy advertising plan.

As if starting a business wasn't enough, this was also when I was asked to teach. Over the next few years, I taught design classes at

Jenny's Career Map

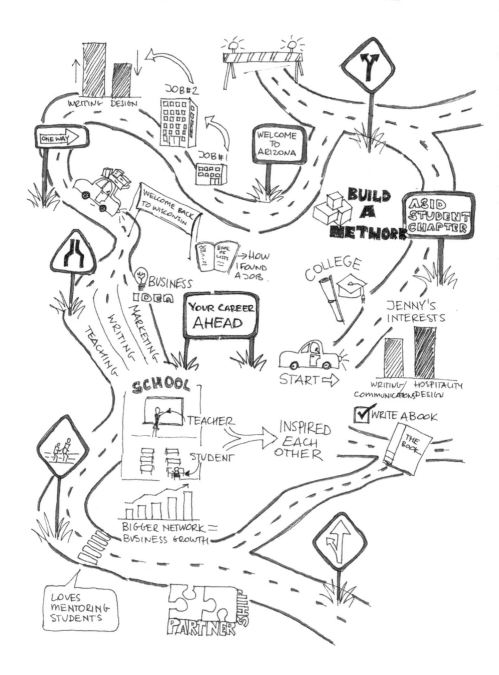

Milwaukee Area Technical College (MATC) and Waukesha County Technical College (WCTC) while building my business. The irony of this story is that when I was in Arizona, I had decided to go to grad school at ASU, so that I could write about and teach design. A job change made it too difficult to juggle both, so even though I was accepted and even enrolled in my first class, I had to let that opportunity pass by. And here I was years later, writing about and teaching design. (This timing is how Aga came into my life, and you are all experiencing the results of that important connection.)

I loved teaching, but my accountant made it pretty clear that it was distracting me from building my business. Unfortunately, he was right. After I stopped teaching, I doubled my business in one year. I have been an entrepreneur now for more than 12 years. This career decision made self-analysis necessary on an ongoing basis. I was carving a niche for myself, and succeeding, even though the recession was paralyzing the industry. But, there is always room for growth, and in 2012, I partnered with a marketing professional, Nicole Davis, and named this new business venture PushPoint Marketing. Committing to a partnership is a serious decision, especially after you have been on your own for so long. In order to take the business to the next level, I needed to make a change and we had talked about teaming up for years–2012 was the right time to make this change.

As PushPoint Marketing, we live and breathe the world of design. Our clients are architects, designers, developers and contractors. We work with people and products that impact the built environment. My design background and hands-on experience are at the core of my brand and have been throughout my journey. It has been building over time and my network has been expanding. People know I am a writer and a connector, and all of these things combined make up my recipe for *The Brand of You*. My brand is still evolving, and I still question the next step to take. My business partner and I

Bill's Career Map

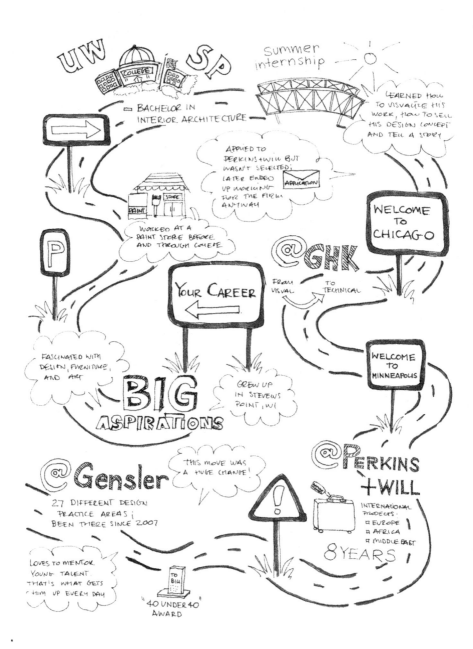

constantly think about what we want to do with our business. We will see where things go from here.

Now that you know more details about my personal journey and my brand, I want to share a few stories about people who influenced me along the way or who simply inspire me...hopefully they will inspire you, too.

Inspirations

The "It Factor"

It is true–I loved school. As exhausting as it is to be a design major, I loved every minute of it. One of the people who made it enjoyable for me was a competitor, partner and friend, Bill Lyons. We compared grades and, occasionally, my scores were higher *(Note: I have to be proud of this accomplishment in my design past, because he is such a design superstar in my mind.)*. We partnered on projects, and we supported each other. Witnessing the work he did in school was when I learned what the "it factor" was.

He was just plain good, and by good I mean awesome. Great ideas and impeccable work just came out of him. He had his sights set on big firms in big cities. I always said that he would design amazing spaces and I would write about them. While I still haven't had the opportunity to write about one of his specific projects, he has designed amazing spaces and received recognition for his outstanding work.

From Chicago to Minneapolis, from Perkins + Will to Gensler, and from one leadership role to the next, he has achieved great things in his design career. I don't get to see him very often, but we remain connected, on LinkedIn at least. He has methodically and successfully pursued and accomplished his career goals, and built a strong and reputable personal brand. He has climbed the architectural firm corporate ladder (currently principal and managing director at

Brian's Career Map

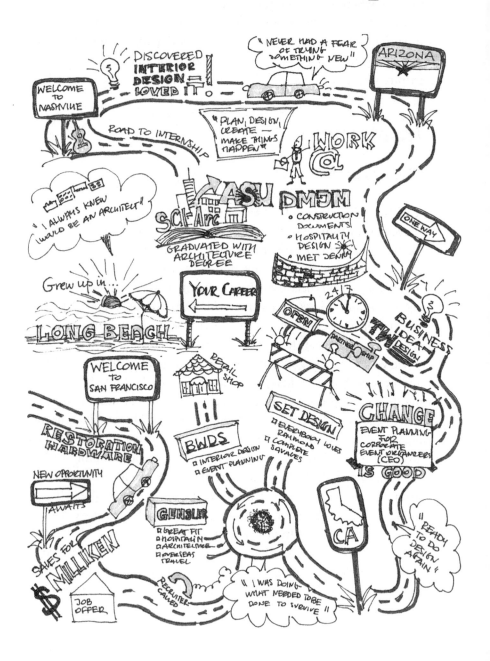

Gensler), and for those who have dreamed about that path, Bill is a great role model. He still inspires me.

The Magic Touch - The King of Reinvention

When I moved to Arizona and started working for a large A&D firm, there were very few people at the company in my age range. Magically, Brian West and I were thrown into a variety of hospitality projects together and helped our boss build a small, successful hospitality department within the firm. He is the kind of person who brightens your day and his creativity goes beyond designing amazing interiors. The right things always seemed to happen for Brian at the right times, and his career has gone in many successful directions.

For a number of years, he achieved great success in event planning. I am not talking little cocktail parties, but rather huge corporate functions and destination meetings. No matter the twists and turns, design has always been in his heart. He has worked as a senior designer with Gensler in California, freelanced as a set designer, worked in residential design and then returned to event planning. He has started his own businesses and worked for a variety of companies over the years in order to suit his life and fulfill his inner need to innovate and creatively express himself.

As president of his own company, LifeStyling (based in Los Angeles), he served high-end hospitality and residential clients while also consulting with Fortune 500 and Fortune 100 clients on incentive and special event projects. More recently, he transitioned into the sales world with a position with Milliken Carpet on his way to working for a luxury brand.

As the Northwest Commercial Territory Leader at Restoration Hardware, he now has a new role and a new place to call home. This opportunity took him from Los Angles to San Francisco, and he believes the many phases of his journey were leading to this position

Robbyn's Career Map

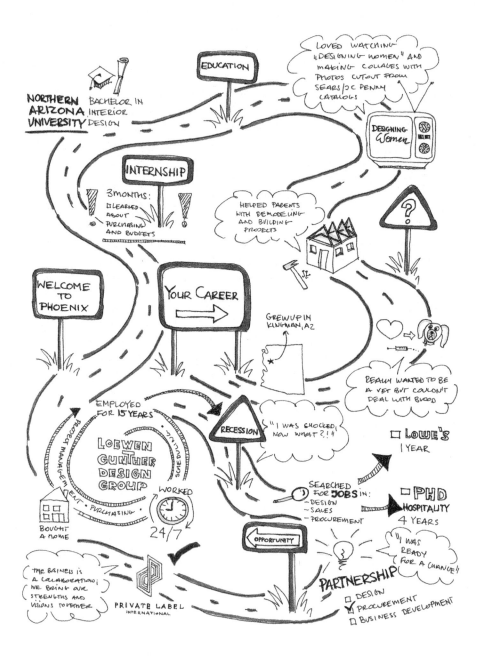

and this moment. You never know what the future holds, but Brian tackles every opportunity and challenge head on. He is the king of reinvention, using his greatest asset–creativity–to take his career in any direction it needs to go.

Special Skills

Robbyn Gabby is a friend and a fellow designer. (She was my room-mate at one time, too.) I worked side by side with her in a creative and chaotic environment, a time in my design career that I will always cherish. Robbyn has many design strengths, but she has a specific aptitude for purchasing and project management. These are design skills that not everyone has, and even those who have these specific skills are not as proficient as Robbyn.

For many years, I tried to get her on the entrepreneurial train. I told her she could build a business based on her purchasing skills. She, like many other designers, lost her senior-level position during the heart of the most recent recession (after more than 15 years with the same firm). She took on a variety of jobs to make it through the turbulent times and, in the end, found a position with a focus on her strengths of purchasing and project management.

Time passed and then I received the long-awaited call from her asking about the pros and cons of owning your own business. Her purchasing skills were being recognized by other small business owners who wanted to outsource that type of work. An opportunity presented itself, and she took a leap of faith.

She is an entrepreneur now, working collaboratively with a few other design entrepreneurs. They have taken the collective company approach to their businesses and continue to refine this model as they grow their client base together. Robbyn's story shows the power of honing very specific and special skills, and that everyone needs to do things in his or her own time.

Jessica's Career Map

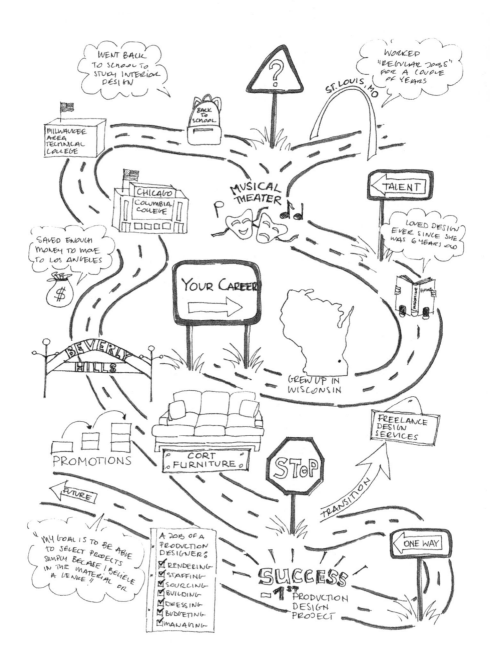

Making an Impression

When I started teaching, I was a little nervous. I wanted to provide my students with valuable industry insights and teach them things I didn't learn in school. As you stand in front of a class day after day, and watch some students' eyes glaze over (or even fall asleep!), you wonder if you are making a difference. I truly wanted to make a difference, but I didn't know I really was until I was told. Before Aga entered my classroom, there was Jessica Mahnke. She told me that I opened her eyes to other possibilities. These words made me feel like I was making a difference and as long as I could positively impact one student, it was worth teaching for a while.

Jessica's influence on me kept me in the classroom for a few years and allowed me to connect with many other wonderful students, who also have influenced me. Hopefully, I have supported their growth and development. I have quietly enjoyed Jessica's success and catch up with her via email and social media from time to time. She completed her Associate Degree in Interior Design at Milwaukee Area Technical College and then went on to receive a BA in Production Design (Film/Art) from Columbia College in Chicago.

She is now a production designer for films, television, commercials and music videos. As a production designer, she develops the visual world that these films, commercials and TV programs exist within. These worlds are envisioned as a result of analysis/research of the time, location, character, themes and tone of the scripted material in conjunction with a director's vision. From renderings to hiring and managing a crew, to sourcing, building and dressing, budgeting and constant management of the overall vision and execution–everything rests on her shoulders.

Ralph's Career Map

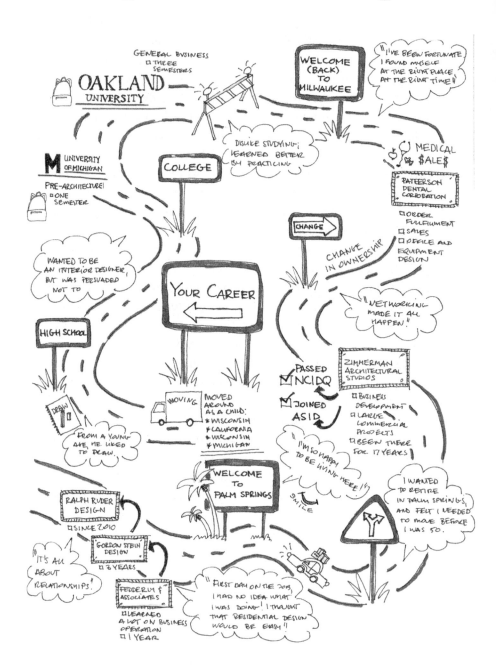

A Strategic Move

After returning from Arizona and taking on the marketing position, I needed to work on expanding my local connections. Over those first few years, my Milwaukee network grew in many directions. Meeting Ralph Ruder was especially enjoyable. He has such an inspiring career story.

Ralph had a hidden passion for design and was able to seize an opportunity. While he does not have a formal design degree, he accumulated the necessary years of experience to qualify for and successfully pass the NCIDQ exam. His design career was firmly rooted in the commercial world and for many years, he worked for one of Milwaukee's top architectural firms. As we met and shared our stories, goals and a few glasses of champagne (I love hanging out with Ralph), he talked about his plans to retire to a warmer climate–Palm Springs, Calif., to be exact.

He was well established in Milwaukee and perfectly happy in his successful design career. Then he started thinking strategically about his future. His 50th birthday was on the horizon and he worried about making a big career and geographical move after this milestone. No one can truly say if things would be more difficult if he waited, but he didn't want to take that chance. Why not relocate and work toward retirement in the area you really want to be?

He decided his future started at that moment. He prepared his resume and portfolio, and began a long-distance job search. One of the challenges that arose was the type of design work available in the Palm Springs area. Not only was he going to be facing a change in climate, he secured a job that would change the landscape of his career–a high-end residential position in a family-owned company.

It takes tremendous courage and discipline to go from a large commercial architectural firm to a family-owned residential business. The type of work, the clients, the way a business is run–it was all different and for someone with Ralph's position and knowledge,

Laura's Career Map

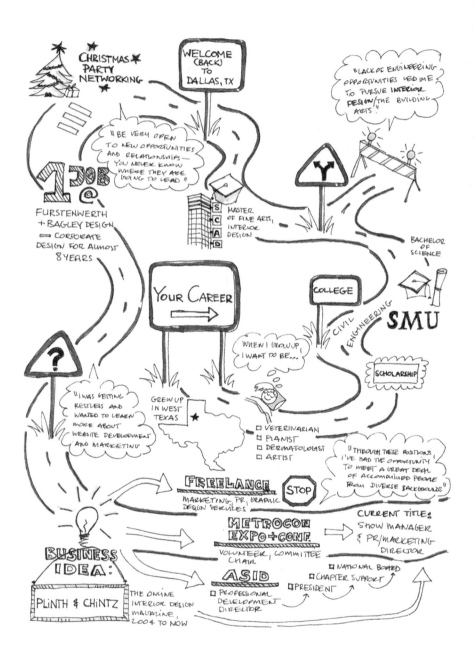

this was a completely new ball game. Of course, he handled it with great poise. Since then, he has made a few career changes and now runs his own business in Palm Springs. I love his story. I hope his strategic move inspires others as much as it inspires me.

The Ultimate Resource

When people question whether you should spend the time networking in the city where you currently live even though you plan to move, I say absolutely yes. The world is an interconnected web of people and you never know how you will connect locally, nationally or globally. A Milwaukee designer in my network moved to Dallas, where she met Laura McDonald Stewart, who was just starting *PLiNTH & CHiNTZ*—a newsletter, website and all around great tool that promotes design education and the transition into the interior design profession. *(Aga and I love Laura and her commitment to the profession, so you will find our article contributions to PLiNTH & CHiNTZ on a regular basis.)* So when my Milwaukee connection moved, it instantly expanded my network to Dallas.

Based on her knowledge of our career goals, she felt Laura and I needed to connect and she made it happen. She was right; it was the perfect connection. Laura needed content, and I needed more outlets for my writing. While our relationship started there, our paths began to cross on a regular basis. We were both involved with ASID and due to our local leadership roles, we would see each other at national conferences. We stayed in touch over the years and I learned even more about her story.

Laura has a degree in Civil Engineering from Southern Methodist University. (In fact, she received a scholarship to study engineering.) Due to the economy and lack of job opportunities post-graduation, she decided to go back to school in order to explore her true passion—her untapped creative interest in architecture and design. She

Jean's Career Map

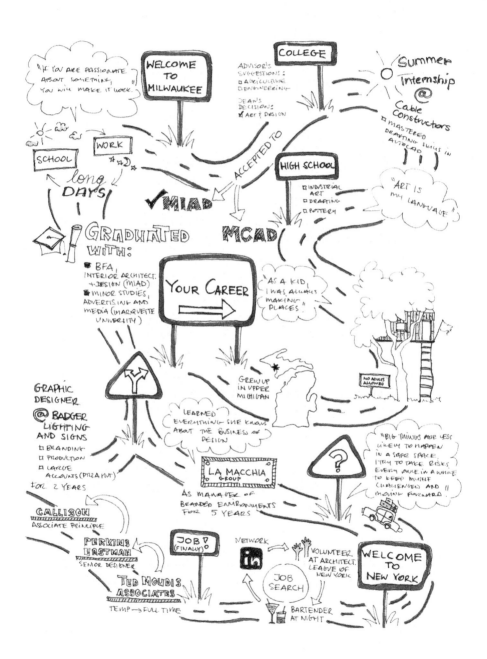

received an MFA in Interior Design from the Savannah College of Art and Design (SCAD). The engineering and interior design combination provided a powerful background and she found great success as a designer in the corporate world for more than seven years.

And then, a feeling of restlessness set in that led to numerous conversations with key people in her network. This period of questioning and self-discovery gave birth to her next career move–and PLiNTH & CHiNTZ was born. Her commitment to creating this resource required some additional web development skills and other knowledge that she obtained. The success of this venture depended upon networking. This endeavor shows great passion and commitment to the profession.

Her success in spreading the word about PLiNTH & CHiNTZ has also nurtured other opportunities. She coordinates a significant tradeshow in the Dallas area called, METROCON Expo & Conference. What's next? You will have to connect with Laura and see for yourself. She is a true networker, connector and resource who in one way or another supports the success of design professionals across the country.

Take a Chance

I get really excited when I hear someone is going to move. I wouldn't be described as an adventurous person–no skydiving or bungee-jumping for me. But a move to a new city, a new career, a new chapter in life? I love it! My move to Arizona was one of the best things I ever did for just me. Some people are too scared to move, or talk about it forever, but never do it. I get so excited for those who take the plunge. It is a special kind of adventure–a leap of faith that takes confidence and commitment.

Jean Chandler belongs to my kind of adventure club. She is a superstar in my book, because she tackled reinvention in New York.

Long before contemplating a big move, Jean was willing to follow her passion. As a teenager, she was advised not to pursue a career in art, but she did anyway. She was committed to obtaining a broad arts education, including skills such as welding. She feels this varied background makes her a more diversified designer. This broad skill set served her well as a designer at a smaller firm in the Milwaukee area, where she had more than a design role. She was part of a team creating branded environments for financial institutions and was involved with business development. She was an integral part of this collaborative team and gained significant responsibility just five years into her career.

She was tackling interesting design challenges and being rewarded with career growth opportunities, but something was missing. Designing in New York was a personal dream, so she moved. When I moved across the country, I needed to secure a job first. Jean was much more courageous. She took a leap of faith and relocated, making ends meet with freelance and consulting work, as well as bartending. She worked on building a network and in time secured a position as senior interior designer with Perkins Eastman Architects. Her hard work and dedication continues to be rewarded and she is a sought-after design professional who was recruited to join the Callison team as an associate principal.

Think About. . .

Do you relate to any of these stories?

Do you want to follow a similar career path as one of these professionals? Then what do you need to do to head in that direction?

If you could talk to any of these design professionals, what questions would you ask? (Write them down.)

Do you have friends or colleagues who inspire you? Do you know their career stories? Ask them.

Ask questions. Listen, learn and grow.

Explore

1. *Windows at Tiffany's: The Art of Gene Moore* by Gene Moore and Judith Goldman
2. *My Time at Tiffany's* by Gene Moore and Jay Hyams
3. *Plan B: What Do You Do When God Doesn't Show Up the Way You Thought He Would?* by Pete Wilson
4. *Women & Money: Owning the Power to Control Your Destiny* by Suze Orman
5. *The Pivotal Life: A Compass for Discovering Purpose, Passion & Perspective* by Jeffrey Wenzler
6. *10% Happier: How I Tamed the Voice in My Head, Reduced Stress Without Losing My Edge, and Found Self-Help That Actually Works—A True Story* by Dan Harris
7. *The Life-Changing Magic of Tidying Up: The Japanese Art of Decluttering and Organizing* by Marie Kondo

CHAPTER 5

Aga's Story

MY STORY BEGINS with a dream. I was born and raised in Ostrowiec Swietokrzyski, a small town in the south of Poland. Every year on my birthday, I would blow out candles on my birthday cake, wishing one wish: moving to the United States one day. Frankly speaking, I had no idea what it would take or how it would happen. I just remember focusing on this one goal and mentioning my goal in conversations to friends and family. Moving to a different city may sound scary enough, not to mention a different country. But I wasn't scared. Somehow, I knew it was my destiny. And so it happened. Two months before I was turning 21, I left home to join a group of foreign exchange students on an opportunity of a lifetime.

While my peers were beginning their studies at public and private colleges back in Poland, I was focusing on learning a new culture, breaking the stereotypes that you are confronted with as a recent immigrant, and becoming comfortable with using a foreign language to communicate socially and professionally. As you can imagine, it was quite a change. Had I focused too much on the long-term plan, the daily struggles would have been much harder to overcome.

STICKING TO YOUR GOAL

My story may be extreme. You don't have to move to another country to prove yourself. Any goal that lies outside your personal comfort zone qualifies as a big one. Thinking beyond tomorrow and outside your reach pulls you out of the ordinary and challenges you. If you asked a personal coach, he or she would advise you to envision the change, see yourself doing a job you want, and be in a place you want to live in.

Have you ever done a mood board that depicts all your goals for the year (a new car, a trip to Hawaii, etc.)? If so, then you know what I'm referring to. I am not saying that dreaming a dream long enough will make it come true. What I do know, however, is that sticking to your goal, living and breathing it, will help you see opportunities that you may have missed or may not have had in the first place.

Sometimes a "one-day-at-a-time" approach is exactly what you need to move forward.

I knew I didn't fit a standard mold. I always questioned the status quo. I never followed crowds, and preferred to make my own path—even if it was up the hill sometimes. Interior design sort of fell in my lap, and I went with it. I had an idea about what it entailed from general studies, and watching my mother rearrange our house frequently. Having been raised in a culturally focused family, I carried (and still do) a high respect for design, art and beauty. My early experiences with dance and theater taught me the value of creativity in all of its forms. I am a proud supporter of the local theater scene, art scene and craftsmanship. Art for the purpose of self-expression and commissioned art both have their place in the world and should be appreciated for what they are. I am proud to play a role (even if it's a tiny one) in this creative world.

Why am I telling you this? Because it matters where you come from, what values you represent and what you decide to do with that background.

Education

It took me four-and-a-half years to finish the program and obtain my Associate Degree in Interior Design from Milwaukee Area Technical College (MATC). Why did it take me so long? I was a good student. But, I worked full time while going to school, which allowed me to gain work experience (in a non-design related field), develop business understanding and grow my professional network even before I entered the professional world. I was also able to pay for school as I went, and graduated with no student loans (a luxury in this day and age).

I remember school very vividly, specifically one instructor (and now co-author of this book!) Jenny Rebholz. She was a part-time instructor, a new face, one of the only instructors with recent design experience. The way she carried herself, her teaching style, undoubted passion for the profession and her experiences intrigued me–and I was hungry to learn more. I jokingly say that I stalked her pre-Facebook by taking every class that she taught. I always came prepared. I did what I could to grab her attention and learn all I could. Jenny might not have known this at the time, but she had a way to push me, to motivate me to do more and better work. I will forever be grateful for that. I will never forget the moment I realized she was more than just a teacher. She changed me. She was (and still is) my mentor and my friend.

Giving Your All...And Then Some

It was Jenny's assignments that made me realize the power of networking. In my Sales Techniques Class, she divided us into small groups and gave us a commercial furniture line to learn about, prepare a design solution around and sell the concept in front of the class. The product we got assigned was called Izzy. It sounded cool, but I had never heard of it before. From one search to another, I ended up talking to a designer at a dealership that sold Izzy locally. She informed me about an upcoming event where the president of Izzy was speaking. So, I went and I met the president. He provided me with a full product catalog and access to the design tool with CAD symbols, pricing, etc. Several years later, I am still a huge fan of Izzy (now called Izzy Plus). And the designer who helped me then is still one of my valuable connections. See how it works? You need to take the first step and get outside your comfort zone. Pick up the phone and call. Introduce yourself. Ask for help. Take a chance and you never know what good can come out of it.

Experience

It was my early networking that helped me secure an internship and job opportunities when I was ready for them. Since I worked in a non-design-related field all through school, I was eager to finally enter the design industry. I didn't know what I wanted to do, but I was ready to learn. Right before graduation, I took a part-time position at a high-end home accent showroom, and a concurrent six-month internship at a senior living company. I quickly learned the differences between a small, residential business, on one side (pricing, market base, timelines) and a corporate, healthcare operation on the other (design process, decision-making, management and team structure). I also discovered that in order to pursue my hobbies and have a life, a retail-based position would be hard to keep. And, frankly, I hated being on my feet all day long. So, after about a year, I terminated my employment at the showroom in favor of a full-time interior design position in the corporate world. And I kept on learning–taking on extra projects, additional responsibilities and working within different teams.

At the same time, I maintained my personal brand. I kept up with my website and made sure my LinkedIn profile was updated. And one day in September 2008, I lost my job due to the economic crash. I was definitely not the only one. Along with me, hundreds of design professionals in different career stages were terminated, with a grim outlook on their immediate futures. I was devastated and took it personally (which is what they tell you not to do). My grief lasted,oh, about a day. After that, I went back to my brand, my values and my passion. My career was focused on me again. And what I wanted was a challenge; I wanted to be in control of my future. I was interested in doing design my way, and offering affordable design solutions to customers who would otherwise not be able to have that chance. Thus, my business was born.

Entrepreneurship

What a journey! In six years, I transplanted myself from Poland to Wisconsin, I learned to live in a new culture, speak a new language,

BUILDING A NETWORK

When I moved to the United States, I knew no one. Well, almost no one. I knew a few of my extended family members, who lived on both coasts, my host-family and my school counselor. That makes a network of less than 10. Not very big, I know. But I persevered.

Over a decade later, I have grown my network to a point where it is hard for me to leave the house and not run into a familiar face. Of course, it helps that I live in a medium-sized city (Milwaukee), but that's not the point.

The point is that I made it my personal mission to meet people, via networking groups and volunteering in neighborhood and design organizations. For a while, Jenny and I had a running competition on the number of people we each were connected to on LinkedIn. Don't be fooled—a strong network is not about the size. It's the strength of your connections that matters most.

obtained a college degree, worked for a few companies and was now starting a business. On a personal front, I made new friends, got married and bought a house. My life was finally falling into place. When I lost my comfortable position in a large firm that offered healthcare, sick pay and two weeks of vacation, it wasn't really a "loss" for me—it was a change. A change toward a goal that's been shaping inside me for a while. Part of being an entrepreneur is seeing obstacles as challenges and using them to make something new. It also means understanding that a path to success is never a straight line, and being comfortable and ready to adjust when necessary while staying focused on the goal.

My goal has been to inspire and empower interior designers in their career paths. I am passionate about interior design, but I see myself in a leadership role rather than a practitioner role moving forward. That's why I do what I do. I have been a volunteer for the American Society of Interior Designers (ASID) since I was a student, not because my employer paid for the membership, but because I saw the immense power an organized group of professionals can have—and I needed a platform within which I could give back. I blog because I want to share examples of great interiors with not just designers, but also the public. The better the public understands what we do, the stronger the industry, the healthier the job market and the happier everyone will be. I make T-shirts for creatives (under the name Enough Said Company—check us out!), because it's a fun way to connect with other creatives and (again) promote the interior design industry. I have co-written this book because I feel a strong need to help others.

This book is about showing you that you have the power to do anything and be anyone you set out to be. You just need to try. It may take more than one try, but it is possible. It sounds a little like a message you might have heard in kindergarten during Career Day. We are here to say that this message does not get old. In fact, you should keep it in the forefront of your mind throughout your career.

Aga's Career Map

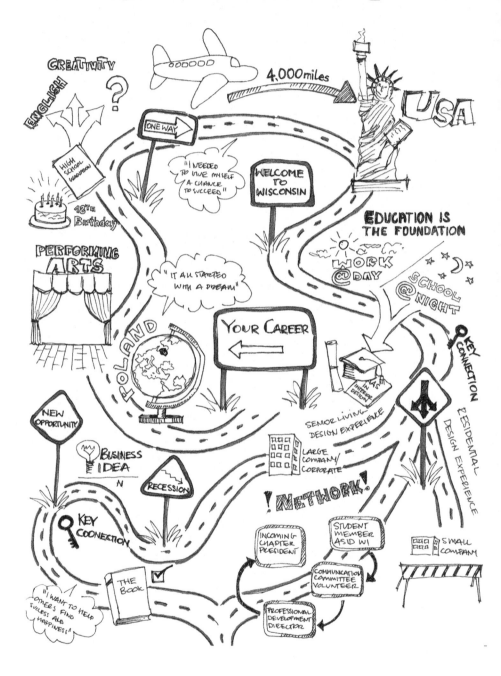

Get ready for a career full of stops, starts and turns. No longer will you have the luxury of holding a job from graduation to retirement. It will be up to you to figure out when to change gears, how to adjust and how to remain happy in this process. The following stories are great examples of such behavior. Perhaps one of them will resonate with you, as they have with me.

Inspirations

Always Love What You Do

The best thing you can do early on in your career is to surround yourself with mentors. Sandy Weber was a principal at one of the biggest architectural firms in Milwaukee when I met her. Only recently did I learn her professional story, which is a great example of how careers are non-linear. Sandy started her education at a technical college and continued her studies at the University of Wisconsin-Stout, where she graduated with a Bachelor's Degree in Interior Design. She knew moving to a "big city" (Minneapolis, in her case) would provide her with a greater range of career options, so she did just that. Sandy started her professional experience working for flooring, paint and drapery showrooms. "Those years were important in building my people and sales skills," she says.

Ultimately, life brought her back to Wisconsin. From architectural firms to furniture dealerships, Sandy tried a variety of work environments and ended up craving the structure of a team-focused architectural firm the most. She climbed the company ranks to become a principal. She loved design and her job every moment of the way. In addition to staying current on technology and design trends, becoming a LEED Accredited Professional and leading the sustainability team at her firm, Sandy always felt passionate about her customers and their projects. Then, and now, she strongly believes that

Sandy's Career Map

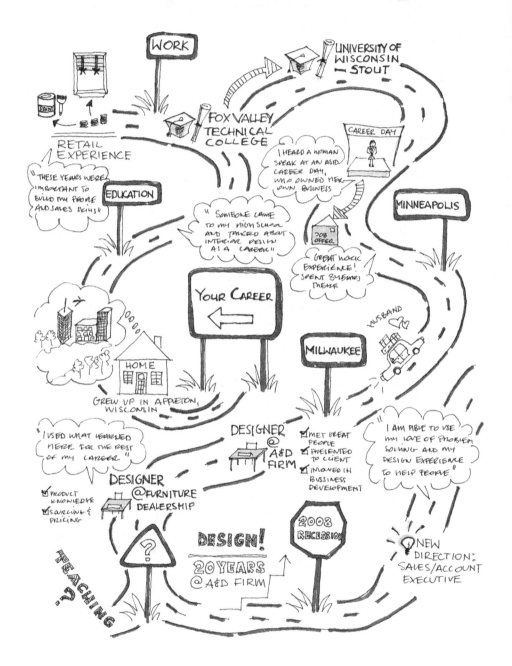

along with good design, one must have great presentation skills to sell his or her work. She was always a "people person" at heart.

"I wanted my clients to feel as if their project was the most important and only project I was working on," she explains. "In meetings, I practiced being very 'in the moment,' not stressed, rushed or hurried, just there for them."

The skills of active listening and building lasting relationships are ones I always admired in Sandy. Twenty years into her professional career, she realized her job was no longer making her happy—it was time for another change. A few years went by, the economic downturn made its devastating mark on the industry and, like many other professionals, Sandy was laid off. "It was a shocking but exhilarating experience," she reminisces.

With her vast network and incredible work experience, she needed to figure out what her next move was going to be. Through a process of self-discovery, research and analysis, she came across a wonderful opportunity that perfectly fit her natural "people person" abilities. Since then, Sandy has held a sales position as an account executive for a wallcovering manufacturer, and is once again loving every day of her job. We meet occasionally to talk strategy and bring a new perspective to each other's way of thinking. We challenge each other, which I appreciate very much. Whether she knows it or not, Sandy has been my mentor and will remain a key person in my network forever.

Chase Down Your Dream

I met Michelle Goertz at a Student Career Day event co-hosted by ASID and IIDA in Wisconsin. She was a student member of both organizations, which she was leveraging to the best of her abilities. Her road to professional success and happiness had just begun. Little did I know she had an important message to share with everyone.

Michelle's Career Map

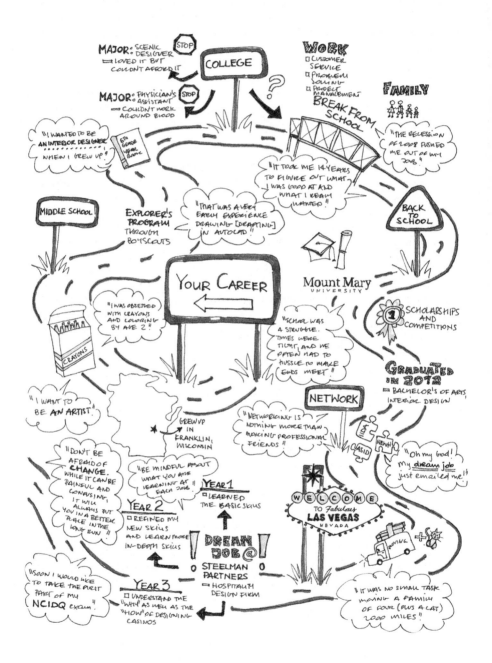

"Until I was 30, my entire career journey felt disjointed and meandering," Michelle says. Even though she knew deep down that she wanted to be an interior designer, life and people around her steered her away from that path. Neither Michelle nor her family believed that her true passion offered enough financial security.

She tried her luck in various customer service positions. Although she learned a lot, that just wasn't it. But as it happens, life gave her the push she needed to act on her dream. She lost her position with a local department store doing tablescapes and assisting customers with their purchases. "I took it as a sign that the higher power was putting me back on the right life path," she says.

So, she enrolled in an interior design program and committed to doing everything possible to graduate and become a professional interior designer. It was a tough four years. The finances were tight. Her family grew from two adults to two adults and two baby boys. In her busy senior year, she generated enough focus and energy to enter a project into the IIDA Wisconsin Student Design Competition (as she had in previous years), and she was awarded the Best of Competition Award, which came with a much deserved and needed monetary reward. Without the prize, Michelle would not have been able to pay for the last two credits needed for her to graduate. She wept as she was receiving the award. Things were finally aligning and working in her favor.

Proud of herself and eager to start working in the field, Michelle enlisted her professional network to find an entry-level interior design position. After eight months of active searching and many disappointments, a member of NEWH, the Hospitality Industry Network, noticed her resume–and the rest is history. Before she knew it, Michelle was moving her family to start a dream job as an interior designer for a leading hospitality design firm located in Las Vegas. She still believes that her story is nothing short of a miracle. But she credits her success to her perseverance, creative problem-solving and, most importantly, the helpful people who made her dream possible.

Stacy's Career Map

"Relationships are important. Nurture them," Michelle reminds us all. Your network, your friends and family are an important component of your success. They can lift you up and help you along in the toughest moments of your life. As long as you know where you're going, they will support you; they will follow you.

Design Your Path

The possibilities are endless if you know what you want. Inspired by a tile designer who came to her high school class as a guest speaker, Stacy Garcia knew product design was her calling. She might not have known the path that she was going to take, but she was focused on this one goal and had determination to do what was necessary to see it happen.

Her professional experience ranged from assisting in product development for Ralph Lauren's Home Collection to being a senior designer for Richloom Contract Fabrics, where she oversaw the textile and pattern design collections for their hospitality division. In those years, she learned not just the craft, but also the business side of product design–licensing, sales, marketing, etc. And when it was time to spread her wings, she did. At 26, Stacy founded her first company, a commercial textile supply company called LebaTex. A few years later, Stacy Garcia Inc. was born and quickly grew into a global lifestyle brand.

I started to notice the brand of Stacy Garcia shortly after graduation. As a specifier of commercial finishes, I noticed it nearly everywhere. Stacy designed patterns for wallcovering, carpet and textile manufacturers–even lampshades. Her style was unique and recognizable; her logo was well known. Her headshot was strategically used to promote both the brand and the products she designed.

And one day, while browsing the showrooms at NeoCon, North America's largest design exposition and conference for commercial interiors, I bumped into Stacy. I wanted to introduce myself to the great pattern designer I had grown to know and appreciate. She, in turn, loved the T-shirt I was wearing (one of our products available through Enough Said Company, which said "Life is too short for beige"). She wanted to congratulate me on a great idea. Seriously? Stacy Garcia liked my product enough that she stopped to chat with me! She even offered product design tips and has since been a valuable connection.

Stacy discovered her passion early on and had the perseverance to make her dream a reality. I appreciate her friendly personality and openness to help a fellow entrepreneur. Despite the tight and competitive world we work within, there is room for all of us to blossom and find success. You just need to know where you're going.

Think About. . .

Have we inspired your next career move?

Do you see any similarities in the career maps?
(If not, look again...)

- Geographical moves
- Key connections
- Changes in a career path

Now is a great time for change. If not now, when?

Explore

1. *Thomas Jefferson: Architect: The Built Legacy of Our Third President* by Hugh Howard
2. *What If...?: The Architecture and Design of David Rockwell* by David Rockwell
3. *Steve Jobs* by Walter Isaacson
4. *Eames: The Architect and the Painter* DVD, Charles Eames (Actor), Ray Eames (Actor), Bill Jersey (Director), Jason Cohn (Director)
5. "Women in Design: Confronting the Glass Ceiling," *Interior Design Magazine*, Sept 12th, 2013
6. "Houzz's Founders Have Become Tech's Newest Power Couple," *Forbes/Tech*, Oct 15th, 2014

CHAPTER 6

Communicating
The Brand of You

WE HAVE ASKED you to spend a fair amount of time soul searching–thinking about you, your situation, and your goals and objectives. As *The Brand of You* begins to make sense and take shape in your head, the next challenge is to put your thoughts into words and create a lasting impression that others will recognize and remember. How can you succinctly communicate your strengths, your values and your differentiators–your brand story? In a quick introduction, an interview or a client meeting, how can you create that wow factor? Your ability to properly communicate *The Brand of You* will give you confidence and prepare you for interactions with others.

Introducing *The Brand of You*

The first step to putting *The Brand of You* into words is creating an introduction. Whether in person at a networking event, on the phone or via email, you need to be able to share a short and succinct description of yourself. This introduction is often referred to as an "elevator speech." The premise being, what can you say about yourself to grab someone's attention during a short ride in an elevator? No matter what you want to call it, your ability to share the essence of yourself in about 60 seconds (or approximately 150 to 250 words) is essential to your professional development and a "must have" in establishing *The Brand of You*. You need to be comfortable and confident sharing your story, so take the time to explore (and write down) different ways to communicate your brand message.

Think about it. If you have a limited amount of time, what can you say about yourself that is memorable? Developing this introduction is the first step toward networking success. If what you say and how you say it is done right, it will open the door to a conversation. If you present yourself in a professional and memorable way, it also will set the stage for an exchange of contact information. It will provide an opportunity for you to follow up with the person via email or a phone call. This first step can be the beginning of a long-term relationship. Years down the road, you will laugh about that moment when you first met.

While you don't want to create a scripted sales pitch that sounds rehearsed or impersonal, it is important to carefully craft this message and practice it in different ways until you are comfortable. Think of answering questions, such as: "What do you do for a living?" "What kind of work are you looking for?" "Why do you want to start your own business?" "What are you really good at?" "What differentiates you?" "What's your story?" By taking the time to outline and prepare this introduction, you will be able to handle a variety of networking situations, as well as have a brief summary that can be used for written correspondence. This introduction serves as the foundation for communicating *The Brand of You*. You will be able to use this summary later as we discuss marketing tactics. You will be able to re-work this message appropriately to suit the marketing tools you select to promote yourself and the work you do.

The following are a few key elements when crafting a memorable introduction.

- The Hook
- All About You
- The Intention
- The Next Steps

By breaking these down into a few parts, you can start writing the section that comes easiest to you. It also allows you to imagine how you would respond in different situations, as well as mix and match the order as appropriate to suit a conversation or a written response.

The Hook

What can you say to grab someone's attention? Can you be more creative than simply, "Hi, my name is…"? Think about a compliment, a quote, a question or a reference that will make the other person stop, listen and respond. You can also think of the hook as an icebreaker. This hook may just naturally come to you as you engage in a specific situation.

We find that compliments related to fashion always work well with design professionals and help segue into more formal introductions and a conversation. Designers inevitably are wearing cool jewelry, dresses, ties, watches, glasses, shoes, etc. And who doesn't love a compliment? While this helps you approach a stranger, it doesn't always result in a deeper interaction. They might just say "thank you" and then pause, return to what they were doing or walk away. It is up to you to turn this approach into a more meaningful engagement.

You can start with something funny, a question, a situational joke or a comment that everyone can relate to (like weather, venue, current events, etc.).

- What did you think of the speaker?
- I can't believe the weather we are having.
- Have you been to this event before?
- How did you hear about this event?
- What was your favorite award-winning project tonight?

If you use a question format for this hook, consider whether it is an open-ended or closed-ended question. If it is closed-ended, the person's response can simply be yes or no. This means you have more work to do to engage the person. Likewise, if you use a comment or a joke, you can't count on the person taking the conversation to the next level. If you use an open-ended question, the person is required to say more in response, which will give you information to work from as you try to lengthen the conversation. You need to have an answer to the question, as well. The person may follow his or her comment by asking you what you think.

Also consider the following: Is someone introducing you? Has someone told this person about you? Are you approaching a complete stranger? Is this person someone you admire? Do you need to interrupt a group to get to the person you want to connect with? Your choice for the hook needs to suit your personality, as this "intro to your intro" sets the tone. It will either entice and engage the person or have the potential to create a deafening pause of silence. Develop a few hooks you are comfortable with, so you can pick and choose the one that best fits the situation.

All About You

Now, share *The Brand of You*. In a sentence or two, you need to tell those you encounter who you are and what you do. You need to do this in a way that sets yourself apart from every other designer they have met with the same level of experience, from the same school or with the same kind of business. This is where you emphasize your strengths and differentiators. Think about the following items:

- Education
- Credentials
- Business experience
- Industry experience
- Notable clients or projects
- Personal interests
- What sets you apart from the competition?

- What problem will you solve and how?
- How will the employer/client benefit from hiring you?

As you compose this part of your introduction, think about what truly makes you different than someone else. It could be the combination of a few of these items that makes you stand out.

You may find yourself in a situation where you have to share this part of your introduction uninterrupted. At certain events or meetings, the organizers may ask attendees to take turns, stand up and introduce themselves. What will you say?

In other situations, this information will be revealed in layers, and the order will depend on the focus of the conversation and/or how the other person is directing the interaction.

- What do you do?
- Who do you work for?
- What is the favorite part of your job?
- How long have you been in the industry?
- What kind of design work do you do?
- Are you from here?

These and other questions will begin to reveal *The Brand of You*, and as the conversation continues, it will inevitably present you with an opportunity to share your intention for this interaction.

The Intention

What do you want? What was your intention for this interaction? Are you looking for a job, an internship, resources or a connection? Sometimes, it is as simple as enjoying meeting new people. As you prepare this part of your intro, remember that your success in getting to this part depends upon how you engage, listen and react to the other person. You have to be aware of how he or she is responding to you and if you can help the other person as much as he/she may help you.

- Subtly or directly, you have to ask for what you want.

- What's the worst that could happen? (Don't be afraid of the word "no.")

Next Steps

As you say thank you, nice to meet you and good-bye, have you identified the next step in the development of this relationship? Will there be an email, phone call, coffee meeting or other follow-up connection? If the person doesn't offer this, it is your responsibility to yourself to let the other person know you will be following up in some capacity. Again, think about how you can make the next steps mutually beneficial, so this interaction has value for both parties involved.

In some cases, the intention and next steps may be combined. We can't cover or even imagine every possible situation or conversation, because it will be unique to every person and every interaction, but here are a few thoughts to help you see what we are talking about:

- *Thank you for taking the time to speak with me. It has been a pleasure meeting you. If you are willing, I would love your feedback on my resume and portfolio. Is it okay if I email that to you? I can also include a link to the website of that new flooring product we discussed.*

- *I am so glad we met today. You have inspired me to learn more about construction and help with that Habitat for Humanity project. Can you help connect me with the committee chair?*

- *It was great to see you again and finally have a chance to have a conversation. I think I know of the perfect venue for your birthday party. I will email you a link to the website and connect you with my friend who coordinates events there. I know you said your firm isn't hiring right now, but if you don't mind, I would like to send you my resume in case the situation changes there.*

While these elements to your introduction–The Hook, All About You, The Intention and Next Steps–all have value, the setting and amount of time you have to share your message will differ from one interaction to the next. Sometimes you may go from one part of the intro to the next like delivering a speech, while other times, there will be an engaging conversation that will take on a life of its own and be less scripted. You need to be prepared for either format, and you need to know your audience so you can alter the message accordingly.

While this book is focused on interior designers, remember that your audience will not always be design educated. A well-crafted introduction is even more important for professionals who don't know you or understand what an interior designer does. What will you say if the person you are speaking to doesn't know the names of local firms, the value of design or what ASID, IIDA or NCIDQ stand for? Communicating your brand to the general public versus the design community will require an altered message. Develop introductions that are appropriate for each one, and that will differentiate you in both instances.

Consider the following tips as you create your introduction:

- **Keep your message short and sweet.** Write, edit and re-write to make sure you delete unnecessary words. Get to the point.

- **Avoid industry jargon.** If you are speaking to another design professional, a certain amount of industry vocabulary is good to establish credibility, but be careful of using too much. If the person is not familiar with the industry, you will have to be even more careful. Big words and industry lingo do not make you sound better.

- **Be passionate about your career goal and the industry.** From paper to reality, your energy should be contagious.

- **Create options.** Remember different people and situations will require altered approaches. Come up with a variety of ways to share your message.

- **Don't say too little or too much.** You want to tell people enough to entice them to ask questions to learn more. If you give up everything at once, they won't need to engage in a conversation and it could seem too self-serving or ego-driven. You want a meaningful give-and-take moment.

- **Plan for pauses.** You want to plan questions and pauses that will allow the other person time to interject. The purpose of this introduction is to help you interact with others, so make sure to purposely plan for these moments. You also need to be prepared if others don't jump in when you hope or if they choose to interject when you least expect it.

While we are focusing on the introduction to *The Brand of You*, you need to keep in mind that you also are representing a specific company (your employer or your own business) that has a brand message to convey. In fact, sometimes your current position and company are a key part of your introduction, especially if you are a business owner. Just be sure that the essence of you is not overshadowed by a company message. Remember, you don't want to become synonymous with the company you work for today. You want to establish a professional brand that is layered with a company brand, so that no matter what happens tomorrow, your own professional brand can carry you through.

THE EVOLUTION OF JENNY'S INTRODUCTION

It is hard for me to remember how I introduced myself right out of school or early in my career. However, I am not too old to remember how I networked as I explored a career shift. I was very focused on finding the right way to combine my design and writing background. At that point in my career, I even had two resumes, one highlighting my design expertise and one that equally outlined my communications skills and experiences. As I met with a variety of people within the design industry (as well as in other industries, such as advertising), this is what I would say:

I graduated from college with degrees in interior design and communications. People have usually seemed puzzled by this combination, but there has always been a clear connection for me. While I also have known in my heart that I would not be a designer all of my life, I knew I needed to gain practical experience to truly understand

what I was speaking and writing about. Now with six years of professional interior design experience, I am looking for a career path where I can combine my passion for design and writing.

When I first started my business, my professional message and company message were one and the same. My business name was my name—Jenny Rebholz of Jenny S. Rebholz LLC. My personal and professional reputations were building that business.

Who is Jenny Rebholz?

I am a designer, writer and connector. The design community is a society of architects, interior designers, fashion designers, engineers, developers, contractors, artists and artisans who do remarkable work. I connect these inspired individuals and support the growth of their creative endeavors. I write about their successful careers and noteworthy projects. I brainstorm, research, listen and learn. I get to

Your Presence

A successful introduction depends on your ability to effectively deliver the message. How you look, feel and what energy you exude all make a difference in the way others perceive you. You may be using the right words, but your attire, lack of confidence or eye contact *know my subject, understand the target audience and then carefully select words to create a story. Every professional and every project has a story. I want to tell your story.*

In many cases my hook in a conversation or in writing was, "I am passionate about design, people and writing."

After nine years in business, it was time to push my company to the next level. I joined forces with Nicole Davis to create PushPoint Marketing. While Nicole and I each have specific areas of expertise that define us as professionals, together as PushPoint we have an equally important mission and message to share.

What is PushPoint Marketing?

PushPoint Marketing is an integrated marketing communications firm focused on businesses that impact the built environment. We are marketing experts, connectors, communicators and strategic thinkers. Our point is simple—we help you connect, create, communicate and execute so you are better positioned to push your business to the next level.

As a principal at PushPoint, I am the Chief Connector and Creative Writer. I enjoy telling stories about companies, projects, industry trends and people. My goal is to help clients elevate their brand and receive the recognition they deserve.

As you can see, the message has evolved with each phase in my career journey. Still, there are common threads that speak to a consistent brand. Each message provides interesting details yet leaves the audience curious enough to ask questions about the design and communications combination, being an entrepreneur, the decision to partner with someone, what type of writing, what type of marketing, the reason behind the name PushPoint, etc. This is just one example of how *The Brand of You* can support your career development.

may be contradicting the message. How you dress, your hairstyle and makeup are just as important. Think about all of these details when preparing to communicate *The Brand of You*.

In the case of a face-to-face introduction, did you consider the following?

- **Your clothing communicates a message.** The style, colors and accessories you choose will either support your introduction and your brand or create confusion.

- **Little things make a big difference.** Brush your teeth, maintain your nails, brush or style your hair. These may be little things to you, but they communicate your commitment and attention to details.

- **Smile.**

- **Communicate clearly.** Think about the tone or pitch of your voice, the speed with which you introduce yourself.

- **Be confident.** This may sound cliché, but it is true. If you believe in your own message, a.k.a. your brand, others will jump on board a lot easier.

- **Body language matters.** Your handshake, posture and eye contact say something to people. Use these to reinforce your introduction.

You Are a Salesperson

If you want a job, a project or a client, you have to sell yourself and your work. Almost any way that you look at it, you have to convince, persuade or encourage someone to take action. You are a salesperson, and the sales process starts with an introduction. Take every opportunity to introduce yourself seriously. Be it a neighbor, a cashier in a bookstore or a fellow designer, don't underestimate any connection. It may start with an introduction and lead into something bigger.

A good salesperson takes advantage of every opportunity. An introduction may be your door opener, but what you do once you walk inside that door is an entirely different ball game. Were you trying to get a meeting with the design director of your favorite firm or a big potential client? The initial interaction went great. You were invited to come in and talk about the details. Now is the time to show off your skills, your experience, your product and really wow them with *The Brand of You.*

Three Steps to Getting Organized

Whether you are preparing for a meeting with one person, an informal small group gathering or a formal presentation, a whole range of emotions can arise and cause multiple levels of anxiety. Organization is the key to tackling this beast. Being organized won't get rid of all of the nerves, but it will help you master the task at hand.

There is a tried and true formula that we by no means invented, but it is extremely valuable.

- Tell them what you are going to tell them
- Tell them
- Tell them what you told them

If you create an outline around these principles, then you will at least deliver your thoughts in an organized manner.

Tell Them What You Are Going to Tell Them

The beginning of your meeting or presentation typically starts with getting acquainted with everyone in the room. Whether formal or informal, people are sharing names and titles, and engaging in casual chitchat. Depending on the situation, you may need to take control of the room or the conversation to get everyone on task. Think about creating a "hook" to get everyone's attention. This may be a joke or

THE EVOLUTION OF AGA'S INTRODUCTION

I secured my first job before I even graduated. That's a comforting situation to be in, but it didn't just fall in my lap. I started to develop my network early on, building relationships and communicating what my professional goals were to people around me. Shortly after, one of my dear connections sent me an internship opportunity, which I applied for and secured. After six months, I was offered full-time employment at the same company. Here is what I said when I introduced myself back then:

Hi, My name is Aga Artka. I am a student of interior design. I go to school at night, and work as an assistant account executive during the day. I'm self-motivated, detail-oriented and I love design.

When asked about my career goal, I would say:

I'm looking for challenging interior design opportunities that support the growth and development of my creativity and talent.

I suppose my initial introduction wasn't all that unique, but my name and my foreign accent (which was a lot more apparent back then) worked to my advantage. At this point, you are probably thinking: "Lucky you, Aga!" Let me tell you something—the grass is not always greener on the other side. In fact, I like the revised version of this saying: the grass is greener where you water it. Being a foreigner, whose name is always misspelled, who sounds weird when she opens her mouth, who doesn't pick up on pop culture jokes and references, I could have fallen into a self-pity mode and chosen to live under a rock. But I did the opposite. I took the weird name and the weird-sounding accent and made it a marketing element. When it comes to differentiating factors, I sure didn't have to look far.

I knew that promoting my brand when I was employed and collecting a steady paycheck would create opportunities in the future. Slowly but surely, I continued to grow my professional network. I became very involved with the local chapter of ASID and got to know the key individuals in the industry. I wasn't looking for employment. Instead, I was interested in creating a name for myself. At that time, I would introduce myself as:

Hi, I'm Aga. I'm a senior living designer, but also have a blog. I write about design, specifically hospitality design. I write about local hotels and also those I stay at when I travel. Did I mention I love to travel?

My early efforts paid off in the end. When my full-time position was eliminated due to the 2008-2009 recession, I was ready to hit the ground running as an independent designer and consultant. In the design industry, people knew me or of me. The challenge then was to introduce my brand to my ideal customer base. I realized that just as I had an interesting story about my place of birth, background and life experiences, others had their own story to tell. The more I traveled and observed the world around me, the more I realized life is about people and their stories. I took that theme and ran with it.s My introduction evolved and became a lot more descriptive. I focused on the benefits of working with an interior designer and the differences in working with me as opposed to other design professionals. In business networking settings, I would introduce myself as:

Hello. My name is Aga Artka. I'm an independent interior designer. I tell stories with space. I help business owners communicate their business brands into a three-dimensional space. I hold a LEED AP credential [I would explain what the letters stand for if I was talking to a client who is not familiar with the design industry] and am a member and a volunteer at the WI Chapter of ASID [same as with LEED, the acronym would need to be explained if the audience was new to the industry].

Sometimes a follow-up question would be asked about a specialty or past projects I worked on. I would always keep it open:

I've completed retail, hospitality, senior living and workplace projects. For me, it's more about the connection with the clients than the industry they represent. If they have a story to tell, they are my perfect customers.

My introduction keeps changing. I adjust it based on the audience. If I'm talking to a potential client, I focus on storytelling, business growth and the impact interior design has on employee retention. If I'm talking to someone within the industry, a contractor, an architect or a fellow designer, I highlight my experience, education and credentials. I try to use simple verbiage when addressing end-users, and more design lingo when speaking to individuals who work in the field. As a self-employed professional, I am seldom asked for my resume. Instead, I ensure that my LinkedIn profile and my website are always up-to-date.

some sort of gimmick to put everyone at ease, make them laugh or stir their curiosity. Your well-crafted introduction may even work perfectly for this moment. This is the time when you want to set the tone and get the parties involved on the same page as to why you are meeting. In addition, it is the opportunity to summarize the points you plan on covering in your presentation or your objectives for the meeting–*tell them what you are going to tell them.*

Tell Them

You have set the stage for what you want to talk about, so now it is time to tell them. This is when you share the important information about you, your portfolio, your design solution or whatever the main topic of conversation is supposed to be. Depending on the type of

Aga

FIRST IMPRESSIONS

When I started my business, I networked with potential clients, but I also tried to make connections in the design industry for possible consulting services.

I remember going into an informational interview with an owner of a furniture dealership in town. I knew this individual from my previous place of employment and wanted to touch base with him to let him know what I was doing—and that I would be available to support his team with interior design services on a per project, contract basis. We had a lovely meeting and, at the end, the business owner commented on my choice of attire.

He wasn't impressed with the fact that I opted to wear denim pants (fashionable, well-tailored, but still jeans) to the meeting. Needless to say, we have never done business together. The jeans may be to blame. I'm not sure. And I may never know. After that meeting, I always err on the safe side when choosing my outfits—I don't want to lose another opportunity to denim!

meeting, you may be dominating the conversation, but you need to be in tune with your audience. Watch their body language, maintain eye contact and keep them engaged. How are they reacting to you? Are you allowing them to comment, question and interact with you? If you feel you are losing their attention, then you will need to adjust accordingly. If they ask a question that you don't know the answer to or request information, make sure you make note of it for later.

Some people start talking very quickly in certain meeting or presentation settings, while others will begin to get off track. Try to keep things short, sweet and to the point. If possible, use visual aids, such as drawings, materials and other "props" to keep things interesting.

Light levels, temperature and other environmental factors may impact concentration levels, so keep that in mind and control these factors whenever possible.

Tell Them What You Told Them

You did it. You finished the main part of the meeting or presentation, so now it is time to wrap things up. You want to make sure they remember the important parts of the conversation, so summarize and *tell them what you told them*. You may want to recap why you got together and the highlights of the conversation, as well as points you hope they remember. This is also when you want to determine what the next steps are for follow up, so you can continue to develop this relationship. A call, another meeting, a follow-up email with information—what is the next step? And, of course, don't forget to thank the person or room full of people for their time and the opportunity.

Preparing an outline and creating notes for yourself will help you feel confident and allow you to be less stressed about forgetting something important. This preparation communicates your professionalism to the other party. So does taking notes during the conversation. While you want to be engaged with the other person, active note-taking demonstrates the importance of the person, the meeting and the information being gathered.

Organizing your thoughts is an important part of the preparation, but it is only half the battle.

Practice, Practice, Practice

Once you have organized your thoughts or maybe even drafted a script of what you would like to say, it is time to practice. Sharing your introduction, walking through your portfolio, describing your design concept–whatever it is, keep practicing and preparing until you feel confident with the material. This could be done alone in front of a mirror or in front of a colleague, friend or family member. The more you do it, the better you will get.

Practice, practice, practice will help you handle the emotional, nerve-wracking side. For a formal presentation, you can practice all day long in front of a mirror, time yourself and do it for friends and family. Don't get locked into a script that will fluster you if one little thing goes unplanned. Be flexible and natural. If you memorize your "lines" like it is a script, you will sound rehearsed and not genuine. You want to have an authentic moment and be comfortable with the subject matter, so you can change course as the conversation does. Something unexpected most likely will happen during your big moment. Someone might walk in the room and throw off your thought process or your mouth might be dry so you stumble on a word or two. You are human. Get over it and move on. You will find your groove again and will finish strong.

As you practice, don't set yourself up for failure, give excuses or say you're sorry. Don't say, "I am really not ready, but here it goes." "I need more practice, but…" "I am going to sound stupid." Just present. If you make a mistake, keep going. Mistakes happen. This isn't about memorization and perfection.

When it comes to the casual conversations and networking, again, practice, practice, practice. You just need to get out there and do it. Make it a networking game. Challenge yourself to go to an event and approach a stranger. The next time make it two, then three, until you are comfortable.

Sell Yourself

Now you're ready. Your introduction and your presence can open d oors to many opportunities. What you do after that is entirely up to you. We've shown you at length what to do to prepare yourself for that moment.

Every meeting, every presentation requires preparation. Interviewing for a job is no different. In fact, the format of a job interview may be frightening to some, but we encourage you to think about it as a discovery session. You should be just as interested in learning about them as they are you. It should not be a one-person show. An interview should not be an interrogation where one side asks the questions and the other nervously answers them. Think about it more like a conversation.

Selling yourself through an engaged discussion is a lot more natural and effective. Be sure you prepare for the part. Research the company and the individuals you are interviewing with. Practice presenting your portfolio. Utilize the presentation method we just taught you. You can shorten it to the bare minimum, but you can hugely benefit from keeping your presentation organized: tell them what you're going to tell them, tell them, tell them what you told them. Don't leave the room without identifying the next steps. Every good salesperson would do that.

Seize the Moment

If you put in the time and preparation, you will be as ready as you can be. It's pretty simple: think about the meeting, presentation or interview, organize your thoughts and spend some time practicing. Remember that no one is perfect and you won't have all of the answers. It is how you handle the pressure, the questions and show your resourcefulness that will make the difference.

We all get nervous or scared at different times for various reasons. Don't let fear paralyze you. Use your fear to motivate you. People who agree to meet with you or sign up for your presentation are not hoping that you fail. They want to learn more about you and the subject you are discussing. You should want to learn more about them. Whether or not you get the job, win the client or receive rave reviews for your presentation, this is an opportunity to connect, interact and promote *The Brand of You*. Be yourself. Be genuine. Be honest. Enjoy the moment, and do your best.

As you continue through this book, you will be introduced to and reminded of ways in which you can market yourself. This chapter has been about developing your core message. It gives you the ability to weave these words into a variety of communication platforms. Whether in writing, in a presentation, over the phone or while networking, you will be developing a language for yourself–you will continue to put your brand into words. As you choose the best marketing tools that suit your personality, communication style and audience, you will be able to adapt and add to this message to effectively communicate *The Brand of You*.

Think About. . .

What's your story?

Take the time to write your introduction.

Did you write your introduction yet?
Practice your introduction in front of a mirror.

Look the part—go buy a new outfit so you feel
confident in the brand you are creating.

Explore

On writing:
1. *On Writing. A Memoir of the Craft* by Stephen King
2. *The War of Art: Break Through the Blocks and Win Your Inner Creative Battles* by Steven Pressfield
3. *The Paris Review Interviews* by The Paris Review
4. *Public Relations Writing and Media Techniques* by Dennis L. Wilcox
5. *The Elements of Style* by William Strunk and E.B. White

On public speaking/oral communication:
1. *How to Deliver a TED Talk* by Jeremey Donovan

Here are two organizations that can help you hone your public speaking skills:
- www.toastmasters.org
- www.pechakucha.org/faq

On professional image and business etiquette:
1. *Modern Manners. Tools to Take You to the Top* by Dorothea Johnson and Liv Tyler
2. *The Gospel According to Coco Chanel. Life Lessons from the World's Most Elegant Woman* by Karen Karbo

If you need a little help with your wardrobe, here is an affordable way to work with a stylist:
- www.stitchfix.com

CHAPTER 7

Networking

KNOWLEDGE AND EXPERIENCE are important factors in your career journey. Depending on where you are on your professional path, there will be expectations of what you should know at a certain point in your career. We are not denying the need to be good at what you do and to constantly find ways to educate and improve yourself. However, in order to get where you want to go, you need people and you need a network.

Everyone has a network; you are naturally born into a network. Your family, friends of the family, neighbors, teachers are all members of your network. While you may not have looked at it that way before, we want you to see that now. And we want you to keep expanding your network. Family, friends, colleagues, mentors, clients, co-workers, employers and others are people who can support you throughout your career journey. For referrals, resources, reputation-building and professional references, you need a network. While you may pick and choose some marketing tools, we believe networking is a requirement. Why? Because success depends on who you know. Who you know and who knows *The Brand of You* will be key to achieving your goals.

Embrace Networking

You have figured out who you are...at least for now. You have put that brand into words. Networking is the most important method of spreading that word–your brand promise. It is a method for exchanging information or services with people and organizations, a process for developing relationships that can lead to proven employment and other business opportunities. Networking is the only way for you to create opportunities to reach your goals.

The concept of networking–and sometimes just the mere mention of the word–strikes fear in some people. This fear comes from the thought of approaching strangers and asking them for something.

Isn't this something you actually do every day? At home, school and work, or at the grocery store, post office, restaurant or gas station, you most likely have to ask people for help with something at some time. You may even crack a joke, talk about the weather or learn something about their personal life. Well, that is networking. Networking is about talking to people and it's safe to say you talk to a few people every day—so relax!

If you talk to people, you have a network. It may not be very large, but it's a start. Every good network begins at home and continues to expand at school and at work. This includes your family, your friends, your classmates, your dentist, your childcare professionals and old high school friends. The people you connect with on a daily, weekly, monthly or even yearly basis are all a part of your network.

Many design students think they are at a disadvantage if they don't know hundreds of design-related professionals. That is simply not true. And many design professionals underestimate the power of the connections they have with the manufacturer representatives, contractors and developers with whom they work on a daily basis. While you will want specific connections, such as knowing other design professionals, to grow over time in order to help accomplish your objectives, every person in your network is valuable. The value of each connection may not be apparent at first; the value may reveal itself over time as you get to know the person better. But until you start talking to the people in your life about your personal and professional goals, you will never know who they know or who their friends' friends know.

So, now that you know you are already networking on a daily basis, embrace it. Just start thinking a little more about the people you are talking to and the connections you are making. Make it a point to really listen. Read between the lines and connect the dots. Start asking more questions and sharing more information about yourself. Share *The Brand of You.*

Learn How to Connect

Some people may be looking for a one-size-fits-all answer to successful networking and we can tell you right now, there is not a 100 percent foolproof method. Networking is a trial-and-error process. Sometimes things work out and sometimes they don't. Sometimes your high expectations will result in disappointments and other times, your low expectations will yield unexpected rewards. We want to help those filled with fear to become comfortable networking and hopefully provide networking pros with additional tips and tricks, or just reassurance that they are on the right track.

Finding Quality Connections

While networking with people who are like you and have similar interests and backgrounds can make connecting easier, you also need people who provide expertise in areas not so familiar to you. Sometimes these people, the ones who operate in a professional world foreign to you, can create the most interesting and beneficial connections that truly expand and diversify your network.

> *"Networking with peer professionals has been so helpful to me. Sharing experiences, sources, situations and so on. Priceless. I try to meet with any and all vendors who call, as they usually have knowledge of the industry from climate to trends."*
>
> — Ralph Ruder
> *Owner*
> Ralph Ruder Design–Palm Springs, Calif.

Meeting new people means getting out of your comfort zone. Go where professionals mingle and network. Go physically or enter a conversation online. If you are searching for employment, join professional organizations that focus on the niche markets you are interested in. If you are looking for new clients or projects, or want to promote your new business venture, look for sister organizations that could complement what you offer. There are opportunities locally, regionally and nationally to make valuable connections through professional and charitable organizations, as well as formal networking groups. Remember to keep your interactions diverse.

Here are several lists of organizations for you to consider:

Interior Design Professional Associations:
- American Academy of Healthcare Interior Design (AAHID)
- American Society of Interior Designers (ASID)
- Association of Registered Interior Designers of Ontario (ARIDO)
- The Center for Health Design (CHD)
- Construction Specification Institute (CSI)
- International Interior Design Association (IIDA)
- Interior Designers of Canada (IDC)
- Interior Design Educators Council (IDEC)
- Interior Design Professional Associations
- National Kitchen and Bath Association (NKBA)
- Organization of Black Designers (OBD)
- The Planning and Visual Education Partnership (PAVE)
- Retail Design Institute (RDI)
- Shop! (formerly A.R.E. and POPAI)

Other Design-Related Organizations:

- American Association of Advertising Agencies (AAAA)
- American Hotel and Lodging Association (AH&LA)
- American Institute of Architects (AIA)
- American Institute of Graphic Arts (AIGA)
- American Lighting Association (ALA)
- American Society of Landscape Architects (ASLA)
- Argentum (formerly Assisted Living Federation of America)
- Assisted Living Federation of America (ALFA)

Jenny

DEVELOPING BUSINESS CONNECTIONS

When I first started my business, I called everyone I could think of just to tell them what I was doing. I met with colleagues for coffee and lunch. I attended gallery nights, fashion shows, restaurant openings and every event I could think of to connect with the creative community.

My intention at the time was just to get to know more people and to be known in the Milwaukee business community. I also continued to become more involved with the local chapter of ASID. I went from attending events to volunteering for committees to being asked to take on a leadership role. My name and reputation were spreading over time.

All of these interactions provided the opportunity to share my story and tell people what I was doing with my new business. The people I met would introduce me to other people or help connect me with people I wanted to meet. Sometimes there were leads to potential clients, but mostly it was just getting to know a diverse group of interesting professionals.

This process helped me to continue to get comfortable talking to strangers and allowed me to become a resource making connections between the people I knew and the new contacts I was meeting. My reputation as a connector emerged out of this commitment to networking and continues to support my success today.

- Building Office and Management Association (BOMA)
- Color Marketing Group (CMG)
- Commercial Real Estate Development Association (NAIOP)
- Decorative Furnishings Association (DFA)
- Illuminating Engineering Society (IES)
- Industrial Designers Society of America (IDSA)
- Institute of Real Estate Management (IREM)
- International Association of Lighting Designers (IALD)
- International Facility Management Association (IFMA)
- International Furnishings and Design Association (IFDA)
- LeadingAge
- Network of Executive Women in Hospitality (NEWH)
- U.S. Green Building Council (USGBC)

Business Organizations:
- Business Networking International (BNI)
- Chamber of Commerce
- Toastmasters International
- Women in Business groups
- Young Professional organizations

Charitable Organizations:
- The 1% Project
- Architecture for Humanity
- Boys & Girls Clubs
- Design That Matters

- Habitat for Humanity

- Historical societies

- Humane Society

- IDEO.ORG

- Junior Achievement

If you don't see anything on these lists that feels quite right, then start your own search. There is an organization for almost every profession, hobby and topic of interest out there. Don't just pay your dues. Membership does not create a network by itself. Attend events and interact with people. Volunteer, serve on committees or take on a leadership role, so members can learn more about *The Brand of You*. They will see your work ethic, learn what it is like to work with you or for you, and be able to refer or recommend you for other opportunities based on this knowledge.

> *"My secret to networking success is quite simple: show up, engage fully and sincerely, and give more than you expect in return."*

> — Laura McDonald Stewart
> *Owner/Founder/Editor*
> PLiNTH & CHiNTZ - Dallas

Take Action

You signed up to attend an event, scheduled a coffee meeting or have a list of people to call or email. Now what?

Some people can just hit the ground running and take it from there. They seize the moment by working a room, picking up the phone or sending a note. They just do it. Others need more time, encouragement and a plan. It is very easy for such people to find a million excuses not to take action. This is when the fear of the word "no" can become paralyzing. You will never be 100 percent ready for every networking moment, so find a way to accept that.

Consider the following suggestions, move past the fear and then just do it—attend the event, make the call, send the email.

Tips for Face-to-Face Networking

- If you are going to an event, you may feel better with a buddy along. Make sure your cohort will support and encourage your networking efforts.

- If you are attending solo, do your research. Who is a member of the group someone within your existing network may know? Place a few calls and ask for people's thoughts or email the person listed as the invitation/registration contact and introduce yourself as a new member or attendee. Most organizations will watch for new members or have a greeting committee who will make you feel welcomed.

- If there is a cocktail hour prior to the program, take advantage of it. Start talking to people early. Most likely, long-term members will introduce you to other members, and you won't even notice when the (happy) hour is over. Always have business cards with you and have them handy. If you have a drink in one hand, be sure you can get to your purse/bag/pocket easily when someone requests your contact information.

- Be prepared. Did you research the company, the speakers, the topic that is relevant to the event or meeting? Be as knowledgeable as you can be. In today's tech world, there are no excuses for being unprepared. Being prepared also means arming yourself with the right tools. Have a pen and paper or an electronic device to take appropriate notes. Don't write notes furiously and forget to engage with the person.

- Use the back of the person's business card to jot down your thoughts after the person leaves, so you remember who it is and how to follow up.

- Give others your full attention–that means turning off (or putting away) your phone. Focus and really listen. Nod and make comments that let them know you are hearing what they say.

- Plan on eating lightly, or even eat before the event. It's hard to have a conversation with a mouth full of food and a plate in your hand.

- If you are having a meal with someone, be careful what you order. Ribs can be messy and you don't want spinach stuck in your teeth.

- If you partake in alcoholic beverages during an event, be mindful of your consumption. Remember that you are creating an impression and representing your brand. Do you want to be known as the person who drank too much, said or did something inappropriate? It could take a long time for people to forget one small incident.

Tips for Phone Call Networking

- Be prepared. Read, research or ask other connections for insight, so you have the background information you need to have an informed conversation.

- Have a goal in mind before you pick up the phone. What do you want? Are you making an introduction, thanking someone, congratulating someone, looking for a job, trying to find a resource or asking for advice? What is it that you want from this person?

- Be confident.

- Be ready to talk and to listen.

- Smile through the phone.

- Speak clearly and concisely.

- Introduce yourself and briefly state why you are calling.

- Can you offer anything to the other person in return? If you are asking for something, you should think about reciprocity. What can you do for this person now or in the future?

- Use the introduction you have been preparing–test it out.

- Be respectful of the other person's time and be understanding if he or she doesn't have time to talk. If the time isn't right, ask for permission to follow up or schedule a time that works with the other's schedule.

- If you are directed to voicemail, leave a message that is short and sweet. Don't rush through your message or your contact information. Repeat your phone number, so the person doesn't have to rewind to make sure it was written down correctly.

- Everyone seems to fear the dreaded cold call, but the thing to remember is that the person you are trying to reach doesn't bite (or at least can't through the phone!). He or she may be the nicest person you have ever talked to. There is a high probability that you will get tvoicemail, but you can't count on that. You have to be prepared to speak to a real person or leave a coherent message.

Tips for Networking in Writing

- Think about the message you want to send. You need to organize your thoughts (Remember **Chapter 6 - Communicating The *Brand of You*?** Tell them what you are going to tell them, tell them, tell them what you told them.)

- Introduce yourself and give people a point of reference, such as where and when you met them previously or heard them speak, who suggested you contact them or something memorable about why you two should know each other.

TAKE A NETWORKING CHANCE

Jenny

When I was just starting my business, I had a goal of writing for national design publications. In order to do that, I knew I needed to connect with people in New York. I started sending letters to editors and trying to make appointments. I also needed to find a place to stay—I was on a budget. You know when people say, "If you are ever in town, come stay with me." Well, I took people up on that offer. I reached out to an acquaintance (she was the graphic designer who created my original logo) and she provided a couch for me to crash on for a few days.

I had several meetings during that winter trip. One contact told me I had to attend the International Contemporary Furniture Fair (ICFF) in the spring. I took her advice and did that for many years to follow. Then, I stopped by the offices of *Contract Design Magazine*. I didn't have a guaranteed appointment. For some reason that day, one of the editors, Diana Mosher, took the time to meet with me. I always joke that she must have been bored or needed a break, so why not meet with the Wisconsin girl.

She looked at my entire portfolio, but said that they didn't use a lot of freelancers. However, she said she would connect me with one of the other editors. We had a nice encounter and I went on my way. I sent her a thank-you email and then, as I prepared for my first trip for

- As part of this introduction, share a point of interest. Something they said or wrote, something you heard about them, a piece of information that will help you show them why you are interested in making this connection.

- Now tell them a little more about yourself and what you are passionate about. Be brief. (You can even include a resume, some other attachment or links to your website or LinkedIn profile for others to look at if they are interested in more information).

- Then ask for the advice, resources and assistance. Why did you want to meet them? Or what do you need their help

ICFF, I reached out to see if she wanted to meet again. It was then that she told me how I inspired her to go to design school. *What?* I had no idea that I had impacted her.

We continued to stay in touch and grab breakfast, dinner or cocktails during my ICFF trips. As the years passed, she became editor of *Multi-Housing News* and asked me to write a few articles. She even hired me to help at a few conferences. She took the time to introduce me to other editors. In fact, she introduced me to Alison Embrey Medina of *design:retail* (formerly *DDI magazine*) and I have been writing for them ever since.

In return, as Diana progressed through design school, I offered tips and advice, and even reviewed some drafting assignments during one of my visits. She is a wonderful friend and colleague who earned a design degree from the New York School of Interior Design. All of this happened because I invested in a trip to New York and followed up with a person who took a few minutes out of her busy schedule to meet with me.

As for the woman who told me to attend ICFF—she gave me a lot of PR advice and, years later, I was able to help her by writing an article about one of her clients.

Take a chance, follow up, be persistent and you open the door for amazing things to happen.

with? If it is job or internship related, be specific about the type of opportunity you are looking for.

- If you are sending an email, send it to one person only and refrain from copying others. Mass emails lack professionalism and tact.

- Spelling, grammar and punctuation are important! These are the details you want to make sure you pay attention to, as the recipient of your message most certainly will.

- Make sure you spell the person's name correctly. And if you are unsure if the name is a he or she, find a way to figure it out.

- Remember your please and thank you. You want the person to know you appreciate their time.

- Is there something you can offer them? Networking is about give and take. Think about what you can do for them or how you will show them your appreciation if something develops out of this interaction.

Follow Up

Sometimes, the greatest impact can be made after a meeting, an event or an interview. How you handle the follow-up demonstrates your level of professionalism. In many cases, a handwritten thank-you note is still held in high regard. In fact, it has gained more respect in this ever-increasing technological landscape. It is a traditional format that shows great respect and thoughtfulness. Carefully select your card stock, pen and make sure your penmanship is legible.

While handwritten notes are good, you may also try sending a thank-you email or a LinkedIn message. Your message should be personal and directed at one individual at a time, rather than sending a group email. You want to develop relationships, so connect with each individual, and touch on something specific and relevant to that person. Taking the time to send a personal note shows you care about making a good impression and referencing details from your conversation demonstrates that you listened. Proper follow-up can have significant impact on the success of *The Brand of You.*

No matter the format, a follow-up message also is an opportunity for you to determine your next step. Your contact might have communicated a time frame for making a decision, asked you to call in a few weeks or stay in touch via email. If that was established, then make sure you do what was asked of you. If you are unsure, then ask for the best way to stay in touch. In some cases, it just may be the beginning of a relationship and it is up to you to determine the proper follow-up.

As a sign of respect, always thank the other party for the meeting/ phone call/opportunity within a day or two. You may, or may not, receive a response right away. Don't be afraid to follow up more than once. People are busy, emails get buried, and so on. Your persistence during follow-up is critical. It demonstrates passion and commitment. You may need to touch base a few times before you receive a response. But, persistence can quickly cross a fine line and become annoying if you aren't careful. Remember to be patient, respectful and understanding. If it is important to you, don't give up...just give it time.

> *"I truly feel that we make our own luck and influence our own timing. You are never going to meet anyone or forge meaningful connections if you are not where others are with whom you can collaborate and/or from which you can learn. The fact that I spent time 'showing up' at different events, volunteering to help out, getting out of my comfort zone and meeting people has made all of the difference in the world."*

> — Laura McDonald Stewart
> *Owner/Founder/Editor*
> PLiNTH & CHiNTZ - Dallas

Timing is a funny thing. The waiting may be painful, but in the end, the reward could be great. It may take years for a connection to pay off or it might happen in the blink of an eye. You aren't in control, but you can be prepared and ready to jump when the timing is right.

As you learn how to connect, practice and continue to expand your connections, keep the following networking words of wisdom in mind.

Give and Take

Networking is about learning, sharing and growing. And networking is not all about you. It is a give-and-take process that hopefully begins with connections and grows into many long-lasting relationships. In many cases, these relationships become great friendships. If we need the name of a great local restaurant to try, we know whom to contact in our network. If we need help with social media, that is, someone else. If we want fashion advice, we have connections for that, too. Finances, check. Real estate, check. Likewise, people contact us for specific reasons or resources. The more you listen to and support the people in your network, the more value they will see in you and the more they will want to help you in return. Whatever your area of interest, specialty or passion, your network will know they can come to you for help. That builds value–and strengthens your relationship.

Be Nice to People

As connected as this industry is, you have to keep in mind that word, positive or negative, travels fast. Be honest and treat others with respect, no matter their title, seniority or position in a company. If you mistreat someone, your network will find out very quickly. So, think before you speak (in person or online). Your reputation is on the line, and you only have one.

> "My one piece of networking advice is to be fair and nice to EVERYONE! It is a small community of industry profes- sionals, no matter how large of city you live in. Years go by and we continue to intermingle with the same people. People change jobs, but relationships continue to grow. It is amazing how intertwined we all are."

— Sandy Weber
Account Executive
MDC Wall–Milwaukee

Quality vs. Quantity

Successful networking is not measured by the number of business cards, connections, fans, friends or likes you have. Networking is a success if you value the contact and he or she values you. It is a success if you continue to build a relationship and even a friendship over the years. You are winning in the game of networking if you are establishing a pool of resources that benefits you and your network. Are you a reliable resource whom others can count on?

Everyone Can Be Good at Networking

Introverts, extroverts, bubbly people, quiet people–however you want to label yourself, it doesn't matter. No excuses. You can network. Good networks are all about variety. Networking can start with sim- ple, quiet interactions with people you know and trust. Or you may find success networking at a big party. Start networking in settings where you are comfortable and over time, you will gain confidence to connect in more challenging situations.

Push Yourself

Networking takes energy. If you are having a bad day, then it may not be the right time to go to that big event you were signed up for. That is okay unless you talk yourself out of those events every time. We can tell you from experience that a few of the times when our inner voices were battling "to go or not to go," and we pushed ourselves to go–*you only have to stay for a few minutes*–were some of the most successful networking moments. So, sometimes you can let yourself off the hook, but other times you need to push yourself, because something great might be waiting for you.

Good Days and Bad Days

Keep in mind that everyone has good and bad days. Someone you are trying to connect with may be dealing with hardship, or is simply not in the mood to be social. Respect the wishes of others. If you are being told that "now" is not a good time, do what you can to accommodate them. Try calling in a few days, emailing the following week or rescheduling lunch for later in a month. If you handle a tough situation with tact, it will reflect highly on you as a professional.

Let Your Connections Work for You

Have you ever tried gardening? It's not as easy as it may sound. There is a lot of consideration and work necessary to see a seed grow into a beautiful flower or a delicious vegetable. You first need to ensure you have quality soil–the foundation. It may take a few months or a few years for your efforts to yield desired results, but it is worth it.

Networking is like gardening. Connecting with people, shaking hands, making that phone call, sending that email–it's all like planting seeds. A connection made today may not come to fruition until months or years from now. It may start with a short introduction, a thank-you note and an email every few months to touch base.

> "Having high expectations of results is the biggest networking mistake someone can make. Networking is a mandatory extracurricular activity for me. I try to do it as naturally as possible and if something comes out of it, great! If not, oh well. There have been times when I took a networking action and was heartbroken when magic didn't happen. It's best to stay positive, put in the time, make it fun and keep moving forward. The object with the most momentum is the toughest one to slow down."

> — Jean Chandler
> *Associate Principal*
> Callison–New York

Maybe you need the answer to a question or you provided a much-needed resource for someone. Then perhaps you attend an event or end up on the same committee. Eventually, you have a conversation about family, travel, or other topic. that creates a common bond. Your seed has taken root and is beginning to grow. A good connection doesn't have to result in a job or something tangible. It could be someone that you admire and contact for advice. It could be a person you know will have the right product knowledge or even be able to recommend a good restaurant for you to try on your business trip.

There will be some people in your network whom you haven't spoken to in years. People come in and out of your life on both personal and professional levels. People you went to high school with and haven't seen since graduation could add new energy and vitality to your network 20 years later.

Every relationship grows at its own pace and needs to be nurtured in different ways. And, of course, there is only so much time in a day. Find a way to keep on top of your network and give yourself reminders to touch base and say "hi" every now and again. Don't just reach out to your network when you need something. Touch base "just because" and check in to see how your contact's life and business are going. See if he or she needs your help with anything.

Networking really is like gardening. Remind yourself to keep planting new seeds each year so your garden–your network–is constantly growing in new and exciting directions.

The bigger your network, the more potential for referrals. You may be the one referring someone or the recipient of a recommendation by others. In such a tight and connected industry as interior design, news travels fast. Whether you are looking for employment, searching to fill an opening or trying to uncover more business opportunities, word of mouth is by far the most powerful way of passing information around. It's like having your own army of promoters out there working for you while you sleep (not literally, but you know what we mean). A referral coming from a past client, a trusted connection or a brand evangelist is the most effective way of marketing–but it also takes the most time to obtain. Why? Because you must first establish a level of trust with your network. The people in your network need to feel confident in you and your capabilities before they recommend you and pass your contact information along to another colleague.

If you are serious about your career, you will approach every networking opportunity with professionalism and respect. What you need to remember is that when people refer you, they are putting their reputation on the line, too. The result of your interaction with the referral impacts multiple networks–yours, as well as the person's who referred you. Are you starting to see the power of networking and referrals and the importance of maintaining a reliable, reputable *Brand of You*?

Think About. . .

When you face a life challenge, whom do you go to for advice? This is a key person in your network.

Is there a person or several people you wish you knew...or knew better? Write down these names so you can strategize those relationship later.

Who is your most trusted colleague or mentor? Invite that person to coffee to practice networking.

Do you belong to an organization (professional, chari-table)? If not, it is time to join one.

If you are a member, are you an active member? If not, it is time to volunteer and participate on a committee.

Have you been on a committee but are afraid to lead one? If so, it is time to stop being afraid and tell people you are interested in leadership opportunities. (Think about being a co-chair if you want to ease into it.)

If you have been an active member of one organization for a long time and feel like you know the key people, then think about other groups to join. What organiza-tions will expand your network in a new direction? Are you looking for clients, obtaining new skills or expertise or just meeting different types of professionals? Pick an organization that suits your objective. Write down some notes so you can strategize this later.

Everybody needs a network. For referrals, resources, reputation-building, professional references and more, a quality network plays a key role in one's professional success. Marketing exposes your brand to new people while keeping your brand visible with those who already know you. In **Chapter 8 – Marketing**, we discuss a variety of tools that will give you the opportunity to take networking to a whole new level.

Explore

On making connections:
1. *Never Eat Alone* by Keith Ferrazzi and Tahl Raz
2. *Networking is Not Working* by Derek Coburn
3. *Trust Agents* by Chris Brogan

CHAPTER 8

Marketing

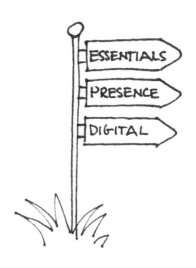

Why Market?

WHY DO PEOPLE engage in marketing? The answer: sales. The goal of marketing is to raise awareness of a brand, product or service. Marketing is way to introduce, build a buzz and enhance the reputation of the brand, product or service. Marketing is part of the sales cycle–the ultimate goal of which is to close the sale. In the case of *The Brand of You*, you are the marketing and the sales team. You are selling a company or a client on the skills, expertise, service and solutions you can provide. But realize that you are not the only one.

Whether looking for employment, thinking about a career change or starting your own business, you will have competition. Setting yourself apart from the competition is what marketing is all about. In order to become known for what you do, sooner or later, you will have to engage in some level of marketing. You will have to let the public know that you exist and that you are qualified and available to provide professional interior design services.

You have been spending time defining *The Brand of You* and crafting your brand message in the form of a well-thought-out introduction. Now, it is time to spread the word about *The Brand of You*. This is the only way you are going to meet people and accomplish your goals. Remember–it is not *what* you know, but rather whom you know. We stand behind this 100 percent. You are going to need the help of numerous people throughout your career journey. To meet more people and get closer to achieving your goals and objectives, you need to spread the word about *The Brand of You*. Put simply, you need to market.

You have options for marketing *The Brand of You*. There are numerous tools available for creating and communicating your brand message. These are the tactics of your strategic marketing plan.

Having a presence (online or offline) is no longer a choice–it's a necessity. It's an expectation. When recruiters search for candidates, they start with the Web. When employers search for talent, they reach out to their network. When clients search for design firms to engage, they use big search engines, not the Yellow Pages.

From print advertising, TV and radio spots and good, old networking to websites, blogs and social media, there is a time and place for all forms. Whether you are promoting a business or yourself, it is important to understand your message, your audience and the reasoning for selecting one tool or another to achieve your goals and objectives. (Refer back to **Chapter 3 - The Brand of You**, if you need more guidance on setting your goals.) We believe you should use well-known platforms to share your passion, spread your knowledge, build new audiences and networks and make new friends. We want you to apply yourself, and genuinely share the message and the story of *The Brand of You* with the world that is out there listening. Here are some guidelines for effective marketing, as well as what we believe are marketing essentials and ways to promote *The Brand of You*.

Rules of Marketing

Life is full of rules, and if you Google "rules of marketing," you are going to find lists of new, brilliant, unbreakable and golden rules. Still, these numerous lists have many of the same ideas in common. Here is our opinion. These are the marketing rules we want you to focus on as you promote *The Brand of You*.

Rule #1 - Be Real

The Brand of You is what you will stand up for and what you will stand behind, so it is important to be honest as you share your brand message with the world. You have to be confident in yourself and present the real you. Be genuine. There is a difference between aspiring to be someone and bluntly pretending to be someone you are not. People like authenticity, so just be you.

Rule #2 - Be Simple

You want people to understand what you are talking about, right? So, keep it simple. Your messages should be concise. Say what you mean and mean what you say. Don't feel like you have to use big words or take three sentences to say what you can with one. Get to the point.

Rule # 3 - Be Consistent

As you select the different tools to convey your brand message, make sure you maintain consistency across those platforms. Just because it is a different tool, doesn't mean it is a different message. You don't want to seem scatterbrained. You want to come across focused and driven. Some tools may allow you to emphasize parts of your brand better than others, but ultimately, there should be continuity in your message from one tool to the next.

Rule #4 - Be Relevant

Know your audience. This is where your knowledge of the state of the industry comes in handy, too. You want to be speaking to the right people at the right time in the right place. You want to be current and knowledgeable. Your message delivery should be appropriate and timely.

Rule #5 - Be Social

While this book focuses on you and *The Brand of You*, marketing and especially participation in social media is NOT all about you. Marketing today is a two-way street. You must pay just as much attention to the message as to the audience you want to reach. Whether face to face, on your website or via your Facebook profile, welcome feedback and discussion. There are real people out there listening, searching for you, wanting to connect. So engage in a conversation.

Rule #6 - Be Nice to People

Show respect to people you meet at any given point, no matter their age, level of expertise or job title. Be nice to people. You never know who and what they know. Reply to their messages. Acknowledge their posts. If you don't have the time to respond at length, send a quick note confirming you received the message and specify when you'd be able to give their matter proper attention. Treat others the way you would like to be treated.

Rule #7 - Show Gratitude

No matter how successful you become, remember to thank those who helped you get there. You can never be too busy to send a handwritten note, an appreciative email, private message or an e-gift. Praise someone's great performance by leaving a positive recommendation on LinkedIn. Spread the love. Your thoughtfulness will not go unnoticed.

Rule #8 - Monitor Your Brand Presence

The key to keeping your brand clean and professional, especially online, is monitoring. You can control what you post, but you can't stop others from posting undesirable photos or content about you. If that happens, ask that the content is removed or your name disassociated from posts when necessary. Keep *The Brand of You* at a high standard. You never know who is looking up your name or asking a colleague about you. Make sure that the content they see is exactly what you would tell them if you were meeting face to face–not too much, not too little.

Rule #9 - Be Strategic

Choose your tactics wisely. Going to market does not mean using every tool possible. You want to choose the platforms that you are comfortable with and the ones that will help you connect with your desired audience. Fully commit to the tools you select. Don't divide your time among many. Give your full attention to one or a combination of tools that will have the most impact. Remember that these tactics should help you accomplish your objectives, so choose wisely.

The Essentials

While there are numerous marketing tools to choose from, we believe there are some essentials for interior design professionals. The essentials focus on image and presentation. As an interior design professional, a certain level of creativity and style will be expected of you. And *The Brand of You* is an entity, so you need to properly represent yourself just like any company–here are some marketing basics that will help you package yourself.

Identity Package (logo, business card, letterhead, note card...)

This brand package begins with a clear graphic representation, a logo or visual identity that reflects *The Brand of You*. You are free to test some designs yourself. It may be as simple as finding a template or selecting the right font style and color. Or maybe you want to create a logo. You may have what it takes to design a stellar logo, but there is also value in involving a third party in this process. If you are starting your own business, you will want to make sure you carefully consider and research the company name and logo. And in this case, we encourage you to utilize the talent and service of a marketing consultant or a graphic designer. His or her objective opinion will pay off in the end. There are freelancers, companies and even websites that offer this service at varying price points. If you are looking to be employed by a company, you may have more important areas to invest your time and money. Just be sure that the graphic representation you choose properly communicates *The Brand of You*.

Once you have a logo you love, use it to design business cards, note cards, a letterhead, envelopes and other materials. Those searching for employment or switching a career path may have a current position and business card. In that case, you need to determine what materials make most sense. While your current position may provide leverage to obtaining a new opportunity, you will still need to present your resume and cover letter on your own letterhead. You also will want to have a professional way to present yourself when you follow up or send a thank-you note. If all of these items are consistent, then it may be worth having a separate business card to complete the package. If you are starting your own business, you will want to invest in the appropriate printed pieces for promoting and running your business. This is not about spending the most time and money. This effort is about presenting a consistent and professional image.

- Put these materials to good use. Take business cards and brochures to every networking event, coffee or client meeting.

- Format resumes, cover letters and references on your letterhead.

- Employers, clients and new connections will appreciate hand-written thank-you notes or congratulation letters.

- If you include a business card in your correspondence, the recipient can keep it or pass it along to a colleague.

- Give extra business cards to people who are willing to spread the word about *The Brand of You*. They will become your brand ambassadors.

Resume/Cover Letter

In **Chapter 6 - Communicating The Brand of You**, you drafted your introduction. Does your current resume communicate *The Brand of You*? Do you have some revisions to do? Maybe you need to start from scratch. No matter your goal, you should have a resume that you are always updating. It is easy to get comfortable in a job or busy running a business and forget to keep this valuable career history document up to date. It is a necessary evil. By keeping an account of your education, experience and accomplishments in one place (printed resume format, LinkedIn profile, Visual CV), you will be able to pick, choose and format accordingly to pursue a specific opportunity. As your career experience grows, you will have to be selective in the information you share, but still keep it documented, so you remember where you started.

For those of you who think you don't have enough design experience to pull together an enticing resume, think again. Just because you may lack design-specific experience doesn't mean you lack valuable skills and expertise. Rethink your past work experiences and the skills required for the job. How can those skills benefit the company you are now pursuing?

Once you decide on the information you want to share, format it in an easy-to-read and organized presentation. Use the resume and cover letter as companion pieces to tell your story. The cover letter provides the opportunity to share interesting and relevant information and establish a voice, tone and personality. The resume then offers bulleted details and data to support what you have communicated in the cover letter. These two documents have the potential to open or close a door to an opportunity. These documents will introduce *The Brand of You*–in many cases when you aren't even in the room. Are you comfortable with the message you are sending?

- The resume and the cover letter allow you to combine the visual and the written brand into one. Does this package properly represent *The Brand of You*?

- Be mindful of the font style and size. You want the information to be clear and easy to read.

- Carefully consider your paper selection so there is a nice contrast, again for easy reading. Unique paper selections can be memorable, but a poor selection can leave the wrong impression.

- Spelling and grammar count. Spell check, proofread and then do it again.

- Have someone else read through your materials.

- Make sure names are spelled correctly, too, or the recipient may not read past the salutation.

- Can you think out of the box and create a format that is different? How does the company you are pursuing present its employees? Maybe that will inspire you. It might be worth trying something new or testing it out with one company or another. You are a creative person, right? Sometimes you need the bullet points, but are there other options to explore?

- "The Objective." Is this a necessary part of a resume? Opinions may vary, but if you are just going to say, "Looking for a position as an interior designer," isn't there a better use for this space? Consider writing a personal statement or using your carefully crafted introduction. This will make your resume different from the stack filled with the same objective.

Portfolio

People are visual creatures, especially those who hire interior designers. Employers and clients want to see what you are capable of. They have read your cover letter and resume, but now they want to see what you can really do. They not only want to see the final product of your creativity–the design solution, your final drawings,

Aga

HAVE A WEBSITE THAT GROWS WITH YOU

Being married to a Web developer has its perks. Ever since I committed to a career in interior design, I have had a website. My husband secured my domain name, set up a simple website and I took it from there. While I was still in school, I used it to showcase my student work and house my resume. As my confidence grew, my website expanded. I added a blog and started to write about design, travel and inspiration found all around me. Even when I was employed by a senior living company, my website was always live, more or less active, but always in existence.

When I found myself jobless, the website, and the connections I made because of it, proved to be the lifeline I needed as I began the next phase of my career. I revised the portfolio-driven website to be more business-focused and added a services page. The graphic appearance of the site evolved, but was true to my original brand. As my brand grew, the website grew with me.

finish selections and project photography–but they also want to be witness to the method behind the madness, your creative process.

A traditional design portfolio was large and bulky. It included architectural-size drawings, a number of 20-inch-by-30-inch sample boards and mounted photographs of finished spaces. The size of a design portfolio is now decreasing, making it easier to transport and show. These days, a portfolio can be as small as 11-inch-by-17-inch, covered in a non-traditional material like aluminum, wood or cork. It can be horizontal or vertical. It can include sample materials, but oftentimes, it just shows photographs and digital images, making a portfolio entirely two-dimensional.

- While your graphics and brand presentation are important, don't let those graphics overpower the important content in your portfolio.

- Be selective. Don't include every project you have ever completed. It should be about quality rather than quantity.

- Be strategic. Select the projects most relevant to the interview or meeting. And organize the order of the portfolio to support your presentation. Don't get flustered flipping back and forth or losing your place.

- If you are not passionate about the project, don't include it. You want to be excited to talk about every detail of your portfolio, as time allows, of course.

- Show your process. How you arrived at the solution is just as important as the end result, and sometimes even more important. People want to understand your thought process.

- Include notes and concept statements. If you are not there to explain the project, can people still make sense of the design challenge and solution?

- Be honest. Was this a team project? What were your responsibilities? Don't be misleading when it comes to your skills and capabilities. The truth will reveal itself quickly.

In today's world, a digital portfolio is just as important as a physical one. You may choose to use any of the popular image-driven social media platforms to showcase your talent (such as Facebook, Pinterest and Instagram). Use school, work and inspirational images or your own photographs to promote your work, yourself, *The Brand of You*. For more portfolio-specific tools, explore the following tools:

- **Flickr** is an image-sharing platform. Organize your photography or original work in folders and share with connections or via social media.

- **Behance** is a rapidly growing portfolio and networking platform for all creative industries. Although it is heavy on the graphic design side, any creative professional can show his or her work here.

- **Dribble** is an image-driven networking site where designers show screenshots of their current projects. It's perfect for graphic and Web designers, but can become very useful to promote any type of creative work. It offers a "Find Designers" section, where recruiters and potential employers can easily discover talented candidates.

- **Houzz** is an online photo-driven database that connects residential design professionals with clients. By posting professional photography of your completed projects, you offer a way for perspective customers (and employers) to experience your design talent and hopefully, hire you when a need arises.

The above portfolio websites are great and fairly easy to use. But the level of customization is rather limited. You can upload project images, fill out a short profile, attach your headshot, but most likely, you won't be able to alter the template, page layout, color scheme. If you set up a Facebook Company Page, it will forever be tied to the Facebook brand; same with Behance and all other third-party tools. If you are committed to developing a solid, customized, digital presence for *The Brand of You*, your own website or a blog is the way to go.

Website /Blog

When it comes to your digital presence, *The Brand of You* needs a base, where all the relevant content lives. It is a place with a unique address, a unique URL. This is where your story is told and your talent is showcased. This is where all the communication channels lead. A website or a blog is the home for *The Brand of You.*

Like a real home, you can either rent, lease or own a home for your brand. When you locate a unique URL that perfectly matches *The Brand of You* (like www.agaartka.com), you will have to decide whether owning the address is important to you, or if a rental agreement is good enough.

We strongly recommend working with a professional Web designer or developer to get that set up. Most domains are rented, and as long as the annual fee is paid to the registrar, you are free to use the domain as yours. There are some businesses that invest thousands of dollars to purchase their domain name, but renting is definitely more mainstream and economical.

Some of you may posses the graphic and programming skills necessary to set up a website. You may choose to dive into hardcore programming code, or use a service that offers Web templates. Whichever route you choose, make sure the page showcases you, who you are and what you stand for. If you are looking for employment, it should emphasize your differentiators and include your resume. If you are switching careers toward (or even away from) interior design, a website should focus on your past experiences and achievements, and your plans for the future. Lastly, if your goal is to start a business, be sure to explain what your unique proposition is. It goes without saying that a website should communicate *The Brand of You*.

For the most part though, interior designers are not Web designers. Let's leave the website work to professionals. Sure, we know a thing or two about color theory and spacial layout, but a Web designer should be enlisted to ensure the website doesn't just look good, but also works well. There are specialties within Web design, just as there are in interior design–people who focus on user experience, accessibility, mobile design and search engine optimization. Your website should follow all the modern requirements and integrate well with modern systems. But, most of all, it should be optimized for the most current search engine algorithms. How good is it if no one can find it, right?

If having a personal Web page falls beyond your comfort zone or budget, consider setting up a blog page, which could act as the digital home for *The Brand of You*. As with website hosts, there are many blog platforms you could use to create a digital journal of sorts. We like to use and recommend www.wordpress.com, but you may find a different one that better matches your needs. A blog can be part of your website or a standalone platform. You may even find a micro-blogging site, like Twitter or Tumblr, to be more practical, given the simplicity and the ease of content generation. No matter the format, what's important is the content you decide to share on there, and then the content optimization.

- Content is king. Tell your story using the exact words you chose to build your introduction.

- Support the written word with images and photographs. Give creative credit where it's due.

- Write something from your own experience, based on your knowledge and driven by your passion. Report a struggle you are going through in school or on a project. Show and explain your creative process. Be honest and be yourself.

- Optimize your website or your blog to include keywords that readers/recruiters/employers may be looking for. If you were an individual looking for this information, what phrase or question would you type in the browser field? For example, if you were a recruiter looking for a designer to fill a senior healthcare designer opening, you would most likely use such keywords as: "experienced, healthcare, interior designer." If a specific skill or experience is required, they would be looking for that term as well. For example: acute care, innovative patient care and evidence-based design. If there is a specific location, it could also be used to narrow down the search. You want to describe yourself (on your website, blog or social media platforms) with the exact words a reader/recruiter/employer would use to search the market with. Know the search patterns of your audience.

There are alt tags, meta tags, title tags, header tags, word count, back links and many more things that can help your content get found. This is a topic you may want to research, but it is a rapidly changing field to keep on top of. If you are really serious about conquering search engine optimization (SEO), then engage an experienced SEO specialist to guide you.

Whether you can hold a portfolio in your hand or direct people to it online, the point is you need a way to visually display your work. You can't simply tell people what you are capable of. In the world of design, you need to show them.

Building Your Presence

While the essentials (logo, resume, portfolio, website) give you a basis for packaging and visually presenting yourself, you have to be more than a cool logo and pretty pictures. You have to connect your brand to your audience. Sitting back and waiting for people to connect with you is not an active strategy, or a successful one. Continue reading to find out how you can utilize various marketing methods to develop recognition for *The Brand of You*, build trust and a following locally, regionally, nationally and globally.

Mail Campaign

There used to be a time when design firms (interior design and architecture) sent out numerous mailings to past and potential clients. Some were promoting projects or announcing newly hired team members, and others were purely social, like a touching-base-type newsletter. The success of this marketing method relied hugely on the size and quality of the mailing list. While electronic methods have grown over the years, some firms still employ this traditional method from time to time. As people receive less snail mail, this printed collateral can help companies stand out again.

While we wouldn't expect individuals to announce a new position or a completed project in this fashion, it may be an option for those starting a business. It is just one of many ways to spread the word and build recognition for your company.

- Visual impact is important. Make sure the piece doesn't get lost in a pile of mail or tossed in the garbage can.

- Carefully craft your messages. Keep them short and sweet.

- Include a call to action. What do you want recipients to do with the mailer or the information you shared? Give them an incentive to buy or invite them to join a conversation online.

- Follow up. A postcard or a newsletter gives you a reason to reach out and connect with your contacts. Make the most of this opportunity. Don't wait for your phone to ring–you should be the first one to reach out.

Advertising & Public Relations

Newspapers, magazines, television and radio–these are the traditional media outlets that are still channels for promoting a business. We would not recommend taking out a half-page advertisement in a local magazine to promote *The Brand of You*, or booking a prime-time TV spot on a local channel. Even business owners should carefully consider these outlets, the audience and the frequency necessary for success before investing money in an advertising program. However, there are ways an individual can use these channels at no or low cost to reach a broad audience.

You want to take the time to establish yourself as a thought leader and connect with editors and program directors, so you may be acknowledged as a source of information for an article or an interview. You may be asked to write an article or one of your projects could be selected as a feature for a magazine. You could even personally appear on the air to provide insight on the subject. This type of public relations effort can take time. You need to build relationships with the right people and gain recognition for your knowledge and expertise. You also may need the help of a public relations consultant if this type of self-promotion makes you feel uneasy. With or without help, you need to find ways to promote yourself or your business in order to accomplish your goals and objectives.

- Identify the media outlets that make sense for the audience you want to reach, and then develop relationships with those editors and program directors.

- Touch base regularly with project updates, photos and other news.

- Timing is everything. Some news outlets need an endless supply of content and stories on a daily basis, while others are working months ahead.

- Be responsive. If you find a media outlet that is interested in your idea or story, get them what they need right away. Be a reliable resource and they will come back to you for more stories.

- Start writing. What are you passionate about? What is your area of expertise? Can you write an article that sheds some new light on a topic? Pitch it to a magazine or a TV station. Do the legwork.

Speaking Engagements

As mentioned above, becoming a thought leader, a key source or an expert in a niche subject can help you gain media recognition. This is a lofty goal, but definitely something to aspire to. There are many professionals in the field of interior design that developed such rapport. Let's play a little game:

- We say hospitality design, you say....
- We say product design, you say...
- We say sustainable architecture, you say...

In your network of professionals, your database of information, you surely have a few go-to connections, favorite design heroes or idols.

You associate them with very specific work. For us, David Rockwell means hospitality design, Michael Graves means product design and Michelle Kaufmann means sustainable architect.

What is your niche market? When people hear your name, what do they think of? Have you considered becoming a thought leader, a spokesperson on a specific topic or niche market? In the world where a heart-touching video or a funny meme can go viral and you may find yourself trending on social media, you too can reach a celebrity status. It's now possible...more so than ever before.

Once you are recognized in the industry as someone with a unique set of skills, experience in one type of project and knowledge of a specific subject matter, schools, organizations, media outlets and conference organizers will look at you as a source of value. To start booking speaking engagements, you must have something important to say about a topic that people want to learn about—that's the ultimate requirement. Of course, it helps if you are personable and energetic, if you know people in the media/magazine/conference world (or have a booking agent) and like to travel. But, without the key part—a topic your audience is hungry for—you won't get far.

The beginnings are always a little up-hill, but after that things will start rolling for you. Look up groups, events and conferences that could potentially be interested in your topic. Form an opinion to industry news and share it publically. Write about controversial topics pertaining to your specialty. Offer to be a keynote speaker at an industry event just to get your name out there.

If you are afraid of speaking in public, it is time to get over it. Most importantly, you must realize that the audience, who very specifically chose your presentation over others, is just as vested in your success as you are. They don't bite. If someone walks out, or leaves a negative review, it's not the end of the world. People's expectations will vary. You can't please everyone, nor should you. Focus on the content, be real, be engaging.

- Search for opportunities online or give organizers a call. See what the speaker requirements are and check on the submission deadlines. Give yourself enough time. Submissions are requested as early as six to twelve months prior to the event, so you have to plan ahead.

- If your submissions are rejected, follow up and ask for feedback. Most often the organizers are happy to help.

- Attend other presentations. Take notes. What makes someone a good or bad speaker? What makes a presentation engaging or boring? Then start working on your plan and performance.

- Once you get the gig, practice, practice, practice.

- All feedback is good feedback. Don't take session reviews too personally. Use the constructive criticism to improve if you want to keep doing this.

- After you present, update your resume with these accomplishments.

REALIZING THE POWER OF ONLINE BRANDING

Aga

I remember this scene like it was yesterday. It was during an ASID WI Chapter event at the Milwaukee Art Museum. A group of us showed up to network and tour a recently opened photography exhibit. I was introducing myself to a few members I did not know yet, saying: "Hi, I'm Aga Artka. I'm an independent designer and the Communication Committee Volunteer." What I heard in return has stuck with me until now. "Oh, yes, Aga...you are the designer who blogs." At that point, I realized that my website, my blog and my social media presence were actually being noticed. People were taking the time to read my stuff, to follow my activity online. I was clearly making an impression on them. I was establishing a unique presence for myself, for my brand, even if I didn't know it at the time.

Award Submissions

Who doesn't like to win awards? It's a good feeling to be recognized. While we don't want you to get consumed with them, awards programs are a great way to boost your reputation and spread the word of *The Brand of You*. There are awards programs for companies and individuals, as well as for designers of all levels. These programs can be project specific or can recognize professional achievements. Completing submissions or participating in design competitions takes time and often costs money, so you need to choose wisely. The submission and competition guidelines will typically outline the cost, requirements, deadlines and promotion opportunities. Some programs promote all of the participants. Some winners are featured in magazines or highlighted at industry events, while others receive monetary awards.

You have to ask yourself why you want to participate. How will the results support the success of *The Brand of You*? And you have to be honest with yourself about the work you are going to submit. For the most part, these programs are not just about pretty pictures. Award submissions are about design challenges and solutions, as well as the impact on the end-users. Packaging a successful award submission is all about storytelling. You need to have the photos and drawings to support a written summary of the project. Typically there is a word limit and, many times, specific questions to respond to. You have to create a quality submission and then wait to see what the jury thinks.

If you are successful, the work doesn't stop there. It is up to you to take advantage of the promotion provided by the competition, as well as to look for other outlets to share your success story. Send a press release to the local paper, send a direct mail piece to your database or utilize social media. It is up to you to make the most of this opportunity and to share the news of your success.

- Search online for opportunities via publications and industry organizations.

- Read the directions carefully.

- Professional photography will most likely be a requirement. Review the image quality guidelines in the directions.

- Don't talk about important details you can't show visually and don't show pictures of details you don't talk about.

- Tell a story.

- When you win, update your resume with these accomplishments.

Digital Presence

Building your presence online can be time-consuming, but it is very important. Once you've secured the basics (the website or the blog), you must have a plan that will expose *The Brand of You* to the right audience. Through the various social networking channels, which should always point back to your website or your blog, you can build a strong brand awareness that will open doors to many opportunities.

Use the following tools strategically. Refer back to your goals and objectives (**in Chapter 3 - The Brand of You**), and identify the specific audience you need to connect with to help you get where you are going.

Keep in mind that technology changes frequently. The tools outlined below, their features and our tips for using them are best known today, but certainly are not the only ones. In a month, six months or a year, there will be new platforms available and current ones may become outdated. The key to remember is this: it's about the strategy, not the tools.

Online marketing brings one more component to the mix–dialogue. It invites conversation, instant access and feedback (positive or negative).

There are multiple ways you can create a successful online presence without a large financial investment. The following pages describe the most popular platforms to promote *The Brand of You*. We hope to help you understand the differences between them, provide user tips and make you comfortable with the idea of joining one or all of them, when you are ready.

LinkedIn

LinkedIn is popularly referred to as a professional networking site. You will not find baby, wedding or lunch pictures here (which may likely be the case on both Twitter and Facebook). Think of LinkedIn as an online extension of your real-life network. It's a living and breathing resume of sorts. In the tightly connected interior design and construction world, part of your value comes from who you know. Show off your network and you can become a valuable player. With more than 364 million users, recruiters love LinkedIn.[10] In fact, 93 percent of them use LinkedIn to find job candidates;[11] 77 percent of all job openings are posted on LinkedIn and 48 percent of recruiters post jobs solely on LinkedIn.[12] If information is power, a powerful network is gold.

- Only 50.5 percent of members have completed profiles[13] (filled in all required information). Having a completed profile makes your profile visible to a greater audience. Spend time on completing your profile to increase your potential to be found.

- Use a professional headshot. No wedding or family event photos.

- Link your own website or blog to your LinkedIn account. Although not likely, you want to make sure that your brand has a home if LinkedIn were to cease operation one day.

- Be specific in your job description. Put yourself in their shoes–include keywords that clients, employers or recruiters may be using to find you.

- Avoid overused descriptors, such as "hard-working" or "self-motivated," in your profile. If you are trying to stand out, use action- or result-driven adjectives, such as "achieved" (and add specifics), "satisfied (and add specifics), "orchestrated" (and add specifics).

- Networking is like dating. You must give it appropriate time to see any return. Daily commitment to your network (by reading updates, checking in with people, commenting on posts, sharing your own or other content) will yield results.

- The best times to post content on LinkedIn are Mondays through Thursdays, between 7 a.m.-9 a.m. and 5 p.m.-6 p.m.[14]

- LinkedIn is especially popular among college graduates and Internet users in higher income households.[15]

- Recently LinkedIn introduced a new feature called Publish. You can now write and publish your own content to your user profile, and start developing a level of credibility for your brand.

- Have nothing new to say? Join Groups and engage in discussions.

- Don't know what to say to a new connection? Pay someone a compliment–about that person's website, recent mention in the media, great article he or she shared. You must be observant and really pay attention in this industry.

- Remember to use LinkedIn!

Facebook

Facebook is an ever-growing social media platform, which started as a college student database. It quickly became an international platform for online socializing with friends and family members. It's a lot more personal than LinkedIn, although you can technically only see updates of those who you know, your approved "friends." As Facebook grows and implements new features, the platform is becoming a much more open, advertiser-focused tool. With more than 1 billion users globally, it is definitely one of the most active platforms for both personal and business use.[16]

- Individual profiles are great, but for business, consider setting up a Page.

- Link your own website or a blog to your Facebook profile. You should also be able to set up automatic sharing every time you publish a new blog post.

- To free up your time spent online, schedule posts automatically. You can do that for up to six months in advance.

- Most people use Facebook between 1 p.m.-4 p.m., with a peak time Wednesday at 3 p.m, so plan your posts accordingly. Messages posted between 8 p.m. and 8 a.m. reach the smallest audience.[17]

- Facebook users are versatile, with an almost equal split between gender, age and nationalities.[18]

- Become a content curator. Share posts/photos/links that resonate with you. By sharing, you are "promoting" yourself and other people/ideas/brands.

- Once a quarter, make a point of reviewing your account settings, to make sure the platform is managed properly and your privacy is protected.

Twitter

Unlike Facebook, which does not limit the amount of characters in your updates, Twitter gives users up to 140 characters at a time to express themselves. Via text, photos, videos or links, you can share content that is searchable by anyone on Twitter. This micro-blogging website can be used to find and follow individuals and companies. Unless a profile is set to "private," everyone can follow everyone. Why is that important? Unlike Facebook, where there is an unspoken rule of "friending" only those you have met before, Twitter gives you a chance to follow updates of people and brands that you have never encountered. For research and networking, that's a powerful feature considering its active user number is more than 302 million and growing.[19]

- Personalize your profile page the moment you set it up. Include a professional photo, so you are not confused with anyone else.

- Once you log into your Twitter account, your Main Page is your Feed Page. It displays all the updates from profiles that you decided to "follow."

- Grow your following by performing simple searches by location, industry, specialty, company name and so on. "Follow" those profiles that are actively sharing new content.

- Engage in conversations and you will start gaining "followers." Mention profiles by using @ and a Twitter handle/name (such as @agartka) if you want to call someone's attention to a specific post.

- To help with tracking conversations, you can turn on notifications (Profile, Settings), so that an alert shows up on your phone or in your email box when someone mentions you or sends you a direct (private) message.

- Manage multiple social media streams in a single view by using applications like Hootsuite or Yoono, or mobile-only applications like Tweetcaster or UberSocial.

- The best time to connect with your audience on Twitter is between 1 p.m. and 3 p.m.[20]

- Twitter users tend to be younger, the largest user group being 18- to 29-year-olds.[21]

- Twitter is great for researching a topic, a city and your competition. Take advantage of it.

Google +

If you have a Gmail account, you also have a Google+ account, whether you've ever seen it or not. That's because Google Inc., the owner of the Google+ social network, lets you use the same login to access all of its products: Gmail, Google+, Google Search, Google Calendar, YouTube, etc. Some of the unique features include Hangouts (a group video chat) and The Sand Bar (a gray update bar at the top of the page, which lets you monitor your Google+ activity, no matter which Google product you are currently using). Although the potential is huge, its current usage rating leaves a lot to desire.

- Having a Google account increases your Google search ranking automatically. So, sign up today and make sure your account communicates *The Brand of You* in the simplest form.

- Google+ reports over 2 billion registered users, only 9% of whom actively post content.[22]

- Google+ users are stronger globally than in the United States.[23]

YouTube

With more than 300 hours of video being uploaded every minute, YouTube is the ultimate source of digital video.[24] It has also been ranked the second-largest search engine, right behind Google Search. [25] It's a social networking platform of sorts, where video is the link between users. In a world where no one reads anymore (or so it seems), images—and especially video—are the ultimate way to call attention to *The Brand of You*.

- Use your Gmail or Google+ login information to sign in to YouTube.

- You can customize your channel name, icon, layout or trailer. Make it your own.

- To see video updates from your favorite channels, "subscribe" to their feeds.

- Optimize the title tag, the video description and the keywords to label the file accurately and increase its ability to be found (searchability).

- According to Nielsen, YouTube reaches more U.S. adults ages 18-34 than any cable network. [26]

Pinterest

It's hard to imagine life without Pinterest—especially for us creative people. It's like being a kid in a candy store—you want to buy every outfit you pin, try every recipe and do every craft project. Pinterest makes it very easy to post, share and like images in all sorts of categories. An image can be enhanced with a detail description and hyperlinks that lead the reader to the source of the information. It is a great tool for building a digital portfolio of projects or ideas.

- Similar to the previous platforms, you can create a personal profile with a short bio and photo.

- "Pinning" means saving an image you found on Pinterest, or an Internet browser of your choice, to your profile.

- You can organize pins (images) into boards (categories). There is no standard way of keeping track of your images. Do what makes sense for you.

- By "liking" a pin (image), you are flagging it, instead of saving it to any of your boards. If you want, you can always go back later and re-categorize it to "pin."

- If you like someone's pins, and want to see their pins in your feed, you can "follow" their specific board or all of their boards.

- 80 percent of Pinterest users are women, the majority of which range between ages 25 and 49.[27]

- Peak time for Pinterest activity is Saturday morning. Your pins will most likely go unnoticed if you are online between 5-7pm.[28]

Instagram

Founded in 2010, and purchased by Facebook in 2012, Instagram has become a social media player nearly overnight. It is a photo-sharing platform that is integrated with Twitter, Facebook, Tumblr and Foursquare (now you can also share 15-second videos). The great thing about Instagram is that it gives all of its 300 million active users a tool to take better photos (and videos).[29] And that makes people happy. Similar to Twitter, Instagram allows you to search users by name or hashtag (#) and follow those who seem interesting.

- Unlike Pinterest, where you can embed a hyperlink into a photo, Instagram photos do not have the capability to link to anything but the home page.

- Also unlike Pinterest, where you can re-pin a photo, Instagram photos cannot be shared.

- An absolute "must" to use on Instagram are hashtags (#).

- Instagram users are predominantly young and live in urban areas around the world. In fact, 70% of users are outside the U.S.[30]

And Beyond

Who can predict the future? There may be entrepreneurs and thought leaders in the marketing, technology and innovation arenas who generate prognoses about the industry; however, nobody really knows how long Facebook will be the No. 1 social media platform. Nobody knows for certain what the next big mobile app will be, and how long that will last before it too gets replaced with something newer and better.

What is your strategy for staying informed? Try subscribing to news feeds from popular sources on marketing, innovation and technology, like www.mashable.com, www.fastcompany.com or www.socialmediaexaminer.com. Tune into YouTube channels of such individuals as Mari Smith (www.youtube.com/user/facebook-mari) or Chris Brogan (www.youtube.com/user/chrisbrogan). Read blogs and publications authored by industry experts, such as Seth Godin, Gary Vaynerchuk, and Guy Kawasaki.

If your interests span all industries and you want to learn about global trends, we recommend *Future Files* and *Futurevision* by Richard Watson. Utilize your Twitter and Instagram accounts and follow those who share valuable insights on these topics (use hashtags #futurefiles, #futuretrends, #innovation #globalissues). And do your own research. You will likely find resources we have never heard of–that's great! Remain open and objective.

With today's mobile technologies, it takes less than five minutes to create a micro-blog post (on Twitter, Facebook or Tumblr), to share a progress photo of your work (on Instagram, Pinterest or Flickr) or to record a short video of a new product installation or a recap from a show you attended (using Videolicious, Viddy, Vine or Instagram). Time is not an excuse. Your comfort with these tools may be a different story. We hope that the above pages clarified some basic usage of the popular social media sites and brought a new perspective on their applications. Focus where it makes sense. Start an account on a platform that targets your audience and matches your goal.

The "You Are Everywhere" Effect

The point of all the marketing techniques we've mentioned is to build a strong and uniform presence for *The Brand of You*. Whether in real life or online, you want to create opportunities for your brand to be seen, noticed and remembered. You want people to talk about you and to see you everywhere. That's how people and companies get hired and that's how opportunities are presented and seized.

Now it is time to bring everything together and begin to create your plan of attack–your road map for success. **Chapter 10 – Time to Strategize** will help you think through the tools you need and the actions you need to take to work toward accomplishing your goal.

Think About...

When it comes to marketing tools, what is your current situation? Here is a list of the tools we mentioned. Check it off if you have it or note areas you need to re-address or improve. And leave the ones blank that you might come back to later. Prioritize your list so you know what you need to do next.

The Essentials
- Logo
- Business card
- Letterhead
- Note card
- Resume
- Cover letter
- Portfolio
- Website
- Blog

Building Your Presence
- Mail campaign
- Advertising
- PR
- Speaking engagements
- Award submissions
- LinkedIn
- Facebook
- Twitter
- Google+
- YouTube
- Pinterest
- Instagram

Do you have a LinkedIn profile? If not, put that on the top of your "to do" list. If you have one and it isn't complete, then spend some time and get that done.

If some of the social media platforms seem overwhelming, then spend a little time watching and learning until you feel comfortable jumping into the conversation.

Explore

On marketing and strategic thinking:
1. *Being Strategic* by Erika Andersen
2. *The Referral Engine* by John Jantsch
3. *Playing to Win: How Strategy Really Works* by A.G. Lafley, Roger L. Martin
4. *UnMarketing: Stop Marketing. Start Engaging.* by Scott Stratten

On resume building and job searching:
1. *Unbeatable Resumes: America's Top Recruiter Reveals What Really Gets You Hired* by Tony Beshara
2. *Resumes that Pop! Designs that Reflect Your Personal Brand* by Pat Criscito

On online branding and social media:
1. *Jab, Jab, Jab, Right Hook* Gary Vaynerchuk
2. *Social Media 101* by Chris Brogan
3. *Content Rules* by Ann Handley and C.C. Chapman
4. *Optimize: How to Attract and Engage More Customers by Integrating SEO, Social Media, and Content Marketing* by Lee Odden

CHAPTER 9

———

Time to Strategize

STRATEGY

STRATEGIZING IS MAPPING. Think of the entire career building and branding process as a road trip. When you set out on an adventure, some of you may have a specific destination in mind. Others may know the direction they are headed, but don't have an identified finish line. If you are extremely focused and methodical about everything you do, you may take the expressway and set out to drive all day and all night to reach your destination. If you are the adventurous kind and more of a risk-taker, you may veer off the main road to experience the unplanned. Or you may carefully plan each moment of the journey and take the longer, scenic route, so you can make frequent stops along the way. Road trips can be a lot of fun; it simply depends on your preference. In most cases, you would rely on a map to guide you where you want to go. In the case of your career, you must make your own map.

We wouldn't be writing this book if career strategy was easy to do and everyone could tackle it on his or her own. As interior designers, we gain an invaluable, process-driven education, but oftentimes forget that our own careers need to be approached strategically in order to meet their full potential. So here it is–we have given you a lot to think about, and now it is time to pull it all together.

Start with You

You have done the work to identify *The Brand of You*. Understand that brands don't happen overnight. A lot of time will pass until you see it fully developed and grown up, but at least you know the important components to focus on. You crafted your introduction and are able to use the right words to sell it to just about anyone. Here comes the strategy part: who needs to know about *The Brand of You*? Whom do you need to connect with? Who can help you succeed?

Identify Your Audience

People make careers possible. People hire people. People train people. People buy from people. We believe in networking so much that we gave this topic its own chapter (See **Chapter 7 - Networking**). Connecting with the right people is part of a strategic approach to career development. In your current position, whom should you know, who can help you reach your objective, who is your ideal customer, to whom should you be promoting your business? Sometimes, it's an individual (specific person at a firm). Other times, it's a group that shares common interests or is industry-specific (real estate brokers, carpenters and general contractors). If obtaining employment is your goal, your audience (company owners, human resources agents and studio leaders at firms you are interested in) is

Aga

IF YOU HAVE AN IDEA, TRY IT

How will you ever know that an idea works, if you don't test it out? When I decided to expand my business into home staging, I did a lot of research to see who the main players in the area were, but no major results returned. I also joined a residential real estate organization to broaden my reach within that industry. I volunteered to speak about interior design and the benefits of staging at organization meetings. I invited individual members to lunch to learn more about their jobs and how my services would benefit them. I saw a potential for staging to become a part of their sales process.

I quickly realized that as much as staging made sense to everyone, nobody wanted to pay for it. Neither the client nor the real estate agent felt like it was their responsibility to take on the expense associated with design time, product cost (whether purchasing or renting) and the actual set-up/staging. In the end, I refocused on commercial architecture and design, and let my membership with the real estate organization lapse. I made good connections, which led to other influential introductions, but no business. Sometimes, you have to try things—not all of them will work out, but it's essential to try.

specific and fairly narrow. If you are researching the industry, your net may be cast a lot wider, and the connections you are interested in may be more diverse. Finally, if you are a business owner promoting a service or a product, you need to identify your ideal customer profile (demographics, socioeconomic status, interests, etc.), so you can target clients through the appropriate marketing channels. That's where the detailed information on marketing (that we shared in **Chapter 8 - Marketing**) comes in handy.

Strategic marketing relies on knowing your brand and your audience. Once you have identified these two parts, you must match up the right vehicle to deliver the message to the right people. For example, if you are a design consultant who identified that your services are best fitted for architects and commercial developers, figuring out where architects and commercial developers do business, where they socialize, which organizations they belong to, what other industries they interact with, would give you a starting point to developing a marketing strategy.

Tactics

With your goal and objectives in mind, now you can focus on the tactics. Tactics are the specific tasks you will perform to get closer to meeting your objective and, eventually, that big career goal. Tactics are the nitty-gritty of the marketing strategy. They are the tiny steps of progress in reaching your objective. Is your overall strategy working? Is it producing the desired results? Is it getting you closer to success?

With the three major goals in mind, we want to show you some possible tactics you may want to consider to get closer to your destination. These are certainly not the only actions you should take. In fact, we realize that everyone's scenario is different, therefore, the strategy will vary. But for the sake of this exercise, we want to show you how to start thinking strategically about your career journey and take control of your future.

Goal: Find Employment

Most jobs in the interior design field are found through networking. Rarely will you see an interior design job opening in the employment section of your local paper. To get hired, you will need to do a lot more legwork. If you are a seasoned professional, this may not be news to you. But for recent graduates and emerging professionals, this piece of advice may be one of the most important ones you will ever receive. Your education and your portfolio do matter and may wow the interviewer, but how you get in the room or on the phone with the person who has the ability to hire you will depend, in huge part, on who you know, who your network knows and how much your connections believe in you and want to help you.

The kind of employment you are looking for may be driven by many factors. Some of you may have identified a specific company you want to work for. It may or may not have an office in your city; you may need to relocate to fulfill your dream. Or you may be unsure about a firm, but know exactly the type of job and job description you are looking for. What if the job you are searching for is not possible to obtain in a city you currently reside? What if your heart is set on a specific specialty within the design industry? Maybe you have grown to love hospitality so much that you only see yourself working on hotel and restaurant projects. You care less about the position and more about the project type. You may be focused on a niche market, such as aviation or senior living. Your healthcare design interest, specifically pediatric, may come from your practical experience in nursing. There are just as many stories, backgrounds and career goals as there are readers of this book. We can't possibly offer you all detailed career strategies to find your career success. But here are a few suggestions...just to get you started.

1) You Want to Work for a Specific Company

Tactic: *Research the company online.*
This may sound obvious but research is a critical phase in building a strategy. Does the company you are interested in have a website, a company Facebook page? What is the company's message, mission? Why did you choose this company to work for as opposed to another? Is what you are finding out still aligned with your own code of ethics and career goal (refer to **Chapter 3 – The Brand of You** for information on self-analysis)?

Tactic: *Search the company on LinkedIn.*
Find out if you are connected to anyone who worked or still works there, or if any of your connections are linked to individuals employed by the company. Send them a message or request an introduction via your connection. Be specific in your request. Why do you want to be linked with someone? What is your goal? What are you trying to learn? People are much more willing to help if they know the specifics.

Tactic: *Leverage your blog or Twitter account.*
Do you have a blog or an active Twitter account? Do you follow the specific company you want to be hired by and other trendsetters in the industry? Write about those companies and their projects on your blog. Mention them in your tweets. You can even go as far as interviewing a designer or an architect currently employed by this company and writing a blog post about that experience. Connect your blog or Twitter account to your LinkedIn account, since that's where those responsible for hiring spend a lot of time searching for information and candidates. Take the initiative to learn about the firm and share your findings. Leave a digital footprint that connects you to the company and the sector it works within. LinkedIn is a great platform to do that.

Tactic: *Connect with sales representatives and other professionals.*
Sales representatives have direct insight into the industry. Since their business is to stay in front of firms and designers, they know first hand which company is busy and hiring, and which ones are not. Start thinking like them. Remember, jobs in the interior design and architecture fields are seldom posted in your local paper. Many firm executives will mention opportunities to their product representatives and consultants, as they prefer to hire based on a recommendation. Be the person who comes to mind when they are asked if they know anyone with a specific skill set, level of experience, personality.

Tactic: *Read the news.*
If the firm you are interested in has been featured in the local newspaper or a national magazine, be sure to let them know you have read the article and are impressed with their work. Via a handwritten greeting card or a post to their LinkedIn or Facebook Page, congratulate them on the accomplishment and even offer to help on a future project. Include a clipping or a link to the article. Let them know you pay attention to the happenings in the industry. Knowing what goes on in the industry will help elevate your professional brand.

2) You Want to Do a Specific Job

Tactic: *Search the Internet.*
Conduct Internet searches using multiple keyword variations of the position you are interested in; utilize popular job banks (www.indeed.com or www.simplyhired.com), recruitment agencies (www.interiortalent.com) and the LinkedIn job section. Find out what the exact position description is and whether it fits your needs.

Tactic: *Research the position requirements.*

Do you have the skills, experience and credentials to fulfill the position requirements? Look into what you need to do to gain the necessary credentials. In addition, you want to find out if the position you are interested in is a fit for you. Don't just look at the technicalities. Focus on growth potential, the culture and the future. (Refer to the list of credentials and certifications in **Chapter 3 - The Brand of You**.) Keep in mind that sometimes the employer will make an exception, even if you don't fully meet the position requirements. People hire people. If they like you and see your passion, they may give you a chance. If you believe in yourself, they will, too.

Tactic: *Search your LinkedIn network.*

Contact your connections (or connections of your connections) that have experience with that position, who are currently employed in a similar role or who hire people for that type of position. Their input may be invaluable.

Tactic: *Be sure that your digital brand is up to snuff.*

While you are looking to be hired, recruiters are searching for you. Update your LinkedIn profile. Know what information people will find online if they conduct a search with your name. Allow your brand to promote you even when you are not there in person. Use technology to your advantage. And remember that you may need to deal with the unfavorable photos or negative comments that you might have not posted yourself, but someone else did. Any content linked to your name impacts your brand. Ensure that that impact is positive.

3) You Are Interested in a Niche Market

Tactic: *Understand the ins and outs of the industry you are targeting.*

If you enjoy retail design, you should educate yourself on the operation, logistics, financing within that industry. Know what makes a store a profitable business, and how design affects the bottom line.

Tactic: *Identify industry leaders.*
Understand who the leaders are in the niche market you are interested in. Research those firms extensively.

Tactic: *Read industry magazines.*
There are numerous magazines that focus on industry niches or dedicate issues to specific niches. Many of them are available free of charge to design professionals. You can request a subscription online. Don't just order an issue. Read it, too. Make note of the talented professionals featured and quotes in the articles. Research their work, their firms, their career paths. Don't just look at the pretty pictures; fully immerse yourself in the content.

Tactic: *Buy or borrow books on the topic.*
We think there is a huge value in owning books that support your professional development, but if you prefer to go to the library or borrow from a friend, go for it—as long as you find a way to continuously educate yourself. Use the newly collected knowledge to initiate conversation in person and online. Be the source of information. Share what you've learned.

Tactic: *Research the keyword.*
Utilize the popular search engines, as well as social media. Search various social media platforms by hashtags (i.e. #healthcaredesign, #hospitalitydesign). You will quickly identify who the active influencers are. Learn from them. Connect with them.

Tactic: *Become a member of specialty design organizations.*
Professional organizations can open doors that will connect you with influential professionals in that field. You should be a member of

NEWH, the premier networking resource for the hospitality industry, if you are into hotel design. If designing retail environments is your thing, be sure to join or at least stay abreast on the happenings of Shop!. Or perhaps you are very interested in healthcare design? Then you should look into organizations such as the American Academy of Healthcare Interior Designers (AAHID).

MOVING TO A NEW CITY

"I had an extensive network in Chicago that essentially meant nothing when I arrived in Los Angeles. The university I attended, the people I worked with in Chicago and the projects I did led to nothing tangible work-wise here. Every initial opportunity I had in Los Angeles was the result of one person I knew who talked me up to someone who was a stranger to me...who then gave me a shot. As much as you hate to hear, "It's about who you know," it's a bit about who you know. No one in this business hires a perfect stranger, even for the grunt work of grunt work. You want to know that the person isn't going to rob you blind when you send them on a run to pick up supplies with your credit card. That being said, it is not that WHO you know needs to be Steven Spielberg or Ron Howard, but rather, someone who sees what you have to offer and wants to see you succeed.

Before you relocate, reach out to everyone you know to share the news—you never know who you know who may have people in that city or, best of all, people in your INDUSTRY in that city. I have worked very hard to get to where I am at in this moment—which is still nowhere near where I aspire to be—but I would never even be here without a cheerleader who saw my hard work and a stranger to whom I could then show my work ethic and skills. This pattern has happened over and over, with the stranger then becoming my cheerleader to some new stranger, and has provided me countless opportunities and allowed the building of the foundation of my career. Thankfully, it only takes one cheerleader to start as long as you maximize your "audition" with that first stranger!"

— Jessica Mahnke
Production Designer
Los Angeles

Tactic: *Once you've done all the research, become a curator of the content on the topic.*

Start a blog and write about it. Set up a Pinterest or Twitter account and share information that can help establish you as a source of information in the field. It's best if you can create your own content, but you can certainly start by sharing information from other experts and people you admire.

4) You Want to Relocate to Find Your Dream Job

Tactic: *Utilize your network.*

Don't underestimate your network. Search your LinkedIn database for professionals who have lived or grown up in the city you are looking to move to. Request a meeting or a phone call with them to obtain their feedback.

Tactic: *Use your professional organization membership to your benefit.*

Contact the local chapter (located in the city you are interested in moving to) of the organization you belong to and explain your situation. People are generally helpful. You can expect a list of resources and names of members who may be willing to help. When asking for assistance, be specific. What are you requesting (information on the city, companies, standard of living and so on)?

Tactic: *Get the local news.*

Find websites for local lifestyle magazines and newspapers. Read them daily. Subscribe to the e-newsletters, Twitter feeds or follow them on Facebook. Through the local news, you can start to become familiar with the names of current or future projects and the development, construction and design firms involved in them. Then, reach out to them. Email the project designer (if you can figure out

CAREER CHANGE-YOU ARE NOT ALONE

"Of course, any individual seeking change will strive wholeheartedly to preserve the sanctity and normalcy in their life, such as their core relationships (family, friends, dog), their regular retreats (gym, hiking trail, coffee house)—these are the places we go to feel community, constancy, comfort. It's where we recharge.

As one seeks to make significant change in his or her life, a darkness can begin to breed doubt, doubt in ourselves. This doubt is like a gray cloud that follows us to meetings, sits above us in the car, sits next to us at the coffee shop and sometimes lays its head on the same pillow we sleep on. We can easily get caught up in the downward spiral of telling ourselves (and believing) that we are not good enough, qualified enough; we don't have the right training, experience, connections; we don't have enough money to do 'it' right, and the list of negative thoughts goes on and on. I've battled this doubt for the majority of my adult life and will continue to do so. BUT, my remedy for pulling out of this dark place is knowing that I'm not alone and that other successful people have been through it and still go through it.

I truly believe that security and stability come from sharing your struggles with a trusted mentor, an equally paired colleague in your line of business who is able to commiserate with you. You need a sounding board; someone who cares for you and wants to see you succeed. Someone who knows what you are going through and will help you carry your burden. Over the last eight years, I've met with another self-employed designer for coffee on average of once a month to talk about difficult clients, visit a new design showroom or industry-specific event, and to just pat each other on the back and say you are not alone. We always leave each other with a renewed sense of being able to conquer."

— Brian West
Northwest Commercial Territory Leader
Restoration Hardware–San Francisco

who it is). Engage online or write a note. Maybe it is as simple as a compliment for his or her involvement with such a great project.

Tactic: *Visit the city.*
Spend a few days getting lost in the neighborhoods that interest you the most. Talk to locals. Don't assume you will like the city just because you read about it in a magazine or someone said you would. Experience it for yourself. Maybe you only thought that you would love Seattle for the cool vibe, coffee shops and bookstores it's known for, but you did not anticipate that the gloomy weather would have such a negative impact on you. Or you may like the ocean, but working and living in Los Angeles would prove to be impossible once you understand the amount of time you would have to spend in traffic getting to/from work every day.

Tactic: *While there, observe company signs at construction sites.*
Call the construction company to identify the designer/architect on the project if it doesn't have a sign up. Contact firms to find out more about them. Do a Google search on them. Explore their websites. Look for articles about them.

The above tactics are ways for you to get introduced and engage with the right people. Once you are able to secure a meeting, an interview or a phone call, that's where your Essential Marketing package (resume, cover letter, letterhead, etc.) comes into play. Of course, you can start the process with sending out a ton of resumes/cover letters or business packages and hope they stick or generate interest. However, we have found that when you want to connect with employers, leveraging your network to identify the name of a specific contact or receiving a referral first leads to greater success.

Goal: Switch a Career Path

Just a short while ago, interior design career options seemed limited to either practicing commercial or residential design, teaching or selling design-related products and services. In the commercial world, a graduate of an interior design program could choose between being an interior designer for an architectural firm, a design/build firm or a facilities department of a large corporation. After a few decades of practicing design, you were promoted to a leadership role where managing staff and clients became more of your focus, not design. A residential design path might mean working under the guidance of a small business owner or combining sales and design skills in a position in a furniture, flooring, window treatment or a kitchen and bath showroom. Alternatively, one could start her own business and offer interior design services to consumers or commercial clients alike.

For those who enjoy an academic environment and want to play a part in shaping future talent, teaching has always been an option. Some people continued from an undergraduate program to graduate school and gained experience as a Teaching Assistant on the path to becoming a professor. Others felt they needed to gain practical experience in the design field before returning to teach.

On the sales side of the business, architectural material and product manufacturers would employ design professionals to represent/sell their product lines. Another option was to sell design services for a firm--be the outside sales agent. Having an understanding of or, better yet, education and experience in the field of interior design was a plus, but the main requirement was the ability to sell.

Career options, such as set design, merchandising, sustainable design, design of branded environments, design blogging and virtual design, did not exist. But today, they do. In academia, the format of teaching is even different now than it was before. Besides traditional classroom settings, you can opt for teaching online, long-distance

IS IT TIME TO START A BUSINESS?

"The answer is not exactly advice-worthy. I've always enjoyed and am quite comfortable working for other people. Economy and lack of job market somewhat forced me into business. After being the last employee standing at my last firm, they hired me as a contract employee working about 20 hours a week. Project offers from other architects and connections were offered and within a year, I was up and running as Ralph Ruder Design. No looking back and I love it."

— Ralph Ruder
Owner
Ralph Ruder Design—Palm Springs, Calif.

◆

"I knew I needed a change to be inspired again, and I knew I just needed to take the leap. I was fortunate enough to have several colleagues who encouraged me. Eventually an opportunity presented itself, which allowed me to become a part of a collaborative enterprise. Timing may never be just right. I just knew I wanted this change to occur. So far so good."

— Robbyn Gabby
Interior Designer/Project Fulfillment Specialist
Private Label International—Phoenix

◆

"I was working for a company in Beverly Hills, Calif., doing upscale model apartments, staging and temporary homes for CEOs, athletes and celebrities. I had been receiving recommendations for projects outside of the scope of my company's services. Despite my proposals to my bosses to use these opportunities to increase their revenue and service offering, they did not wish to pursue these avenues. So, I began taking on these additional projects outside of work. As I did, I heard that inner voice telling me that if what I could do wasn't of value to this company, then I was not where I needed to be. I promised myself that if I got even one large project that could briefly sustain me, I would make the jump. Then I received a call from Maria Shriver, telling me she had seen a model apartment I designed and wanted me to design her daughter's new place. And that was it: I jumped."

— Jessica Mahnke
Production Designer
Los Angeles

or even seek teaching opportunities with digital platforms such as Skillshare or Lynda. The ever- changing industry of interior design is opening up and allowing new employment models to emerge every day. The market is hungry for creatives who can respond to a need at hand. We can't imagine what the future holds for this industry, but we are very excited about the possibilities.

THINGS TO THINK ABOUT WHEN CONTEMPLATING ENTREPRENEURSHIP

"Before making a change, planning is key. Evaluate job enjoyment with real-world factors, such as health insurance, retirement planning, etc. All aspects, whether good or bad, should be considered in your decision."

— Ralph Ruder
Owner
Ralph Ruder Design–Palm Springs, Calif.

◆

"Speak to other business owners—advice and information are always free. No matter what, follow your instinct and surround yourself with colleagues and friends who support you. You are ultimately in control of your destiny, but it always helps to have cheerleaders, a 'you can do it' section. Know what you want out of it and have realistic expectations. You are only as good as your word, your work and your reputation. Network. While digital networking is important today, don't forget a face and a handshake are always more memorable."

— Robbyn Gabby
Interior Designer/Project Fulfillment Specialist
Private Label International–Phoenix

◆

"For me, the yearning to be doing what I should be doing was so strong sometimes that I almost made rash decisions, thinking, 'Oh, it will just work itself out,' even if I am ill-prepared for the landing. (And to a certain extent, my highly supportive family may have been able

In order to take advantage of the newly created design opportunities, you must keep your mind open. You must be flexible and willing to take risks. You must also have a versatile network that can help you identify or build opportunities. No matter if you choose a traditional interior design career path or a less conventional one, your education, your experience and your network will help you along your professional journey.

to be the safety net I would have needed for such an approach.) But, I think living with the restlessness and dissatisfaction that comes with someone else not finding value in what you have to offer can be the best catalyst to effective strategizing."

My best tips for this restless time right before you make the jump:

- Save some money (work and money will always be spotty at the beginning, and will come in fits and starts for even the first year or two until you become the go-to designer for a wide pool of people.

- Attend anything even remotely possible at which to network (getting your face in front of people and having them personally like you/get along with you will go farther toward someone giving you that first shot than any well-formatted resume ever will).

- Look around at who else is doing the things you want to be doing—read about them, meet them, pay attention to what they do and how they do it, and, however possible, get yourself as close to that world as you can...until you get yourself in to and a part of that world. Speaking the language, knowing the shorthand, familiarity with elements critical to the job and the industry will help you seem like an insider until you really are one. No one wants to feel like they are hiring someone brand new (even when they are paying you like you are), and a little knowledge and comfort go a long way when you are a hard worker who pays great attention."

— Jessica Mahnke
Production Designer
Los Angeles

1) Interior Design Is Your Second/Third Career Path

Tactic: *Evaluate your current skills/experience.*
Take a personality test. Or at the very least, go through *The Brand of You* discovery process we outlined in **Chapter 3 - The Brand of You**.
Tactic: *Identify necessary industry-specific credentials.*
Some may be easy to obtain, others may require time to qualify for and obtain. For a detailed list of possible certifications and credentialing details, refer back to **Chapter 3 - The Brand of You**.

Tactic: *Take advantage of your previous professional experience.*
Outline your previous experiences in your resume/cover letter and the digital equivalents, such as your LinkedIn profile. Look closely at the skills you learned and promote them as your differentiators. How can your nursing, retail management or even accounting experiences benefit the potential employer/client?

Tactic: *Attend conferences and events where industry leaders and experts will be speaking.*
Listen to their presentations, take notes and then introduce yourself. Thank them for offering the insights. Follow up afterwards to learn more. It's not stalking. It's how relationships are built.

Tactic: *Become a member of design organizations.*
Use your membership to connect with professionals in the field. Depending on your previous profession, you may have an identified niche market you want to pursue. Immerse yourself in that market by joining an appropriate organization. For example, you may have decided to transition from a business manager role at a hotel chain to designing hospitality environments. You have a vast understanding of the day-to-day operations and want to use that knowledge to develop functional design solutions for hotels. You should be a mem-

ber of NEWH, the premier networking resource for the hospitality industry, if you are into hotel design. On the other hand, you may have extensive retail experience and recently developed more interest in merchandising and spatial design. Becoming a member of Shop! would help advance your knowledge and your network in the design side of the industry. Play your past experiences up, never down.

2) You Are Interested in Pursuing a Non-traditional Interior Design Career Path

Tactic: *Identify your niche.*
If a traditional role of an interior designer doesn't seem fitting for you, what shape do you see your career taking? Which direction do you want to go? How can you utilize your experiences thus far and enrich your position in the future? Are you a good writer and want to start a blog that could grow into a source of income? Or are environmental impact, human health and sustainability your areas of interest?

Tactic: *Narrow down the business model that works for you.*
Do you want to work from home or travel? Are you a computer-savvy, detail-oriented person or is communicating and interacting with people more your thing? We are certain there is a path that will best suit your personality. Creating or discovering it starts with understanding yourself. Refer back to **Chapter 3 - The Brand of You**, for questions that will help you start the self-analysis process.

Tactic: *Talk to those whose shoes you want to fill.*
Reach out to the individuals who specialize in the subject you are interested in. If set design is your interest, search out professionals who do that. Maybe even talk to an actor or a director. Such people work in that environment and would be able to speak from first-hand experience.

Find direct and indirect connections and start asking questions. The more you learn early on, the more information you will have to support your career decision.

Tactic: ***Prepare yourself to start at the very bottom.***
Whenever you make a change, you should be prepared to go through a learning curve. There is nothing shameful about learning. Just know that it's not forever. The apprentice role (to put it lightly) may not be all that glamorous, but it may be critical in your career development process. We all have to start somewhere.

3) You want to teach

Tactic: ***Evaluate your credentials and areas of expertise***
In many cases, pursing a career in teaching will require an investment in your own education. While some programs do hire part-time instructors without graduate degrees, many programs require a master degree.

What are your credentials and what are the requirements of the programs of interest to you? If additional education is not required, do you have specialized expertise that will be valuable to the program? If additional education is required, what schools offer a program suitable to your location, time, interests and finances?

Tactic: ***Get connected***
The Interior Designers Educators Council (IDEC) is a great professional organization for those pursuing an educational path. From networking and teaching tools to information about design programs across the country, IDEC is a great resource.

Tactic: ***Research Academic Programs***
What is the right academic setting to pursue your advanced degree?

There are a variety of degrees and specialties available as well as program options for online learning. What is the right fit for you? And where do you want to teach? Looking at the requirements of the schools where you hope to teach some day may help guide your academic path.

Tactic: *Talk to other instructors*
Reach out to your past instructors or introduce yourself to other teaching professionals. Learn the pros and cons of teaching. The advice of practicing professionals is always valuable.

4) You want to apply your experiences in a different profession

Tactic: Identify the field you want to switch to
We have seen many successful transitions where an interior design background proved to be of great benefit. Your problem solving skills, mediation and interpersonal communication skills and abstract thinking will prove to be assets in many different scenarios. Go back to Chapter 3 – The Brand of You and really think about your strength and weaknesses as well as your interests. We have found that many people uncover new and exciting opportunities based on unique and sometimes unlikely combinations of skills and hobbies.

Tactic: *Evaluate your credentials, education and experience*
Once you have identified your new path, evaluate if you need further education or credentials to achieve your goal. Pursuing this new path may just require you to change your approach to your resume and cover letter. Look at how you can present your design experiences in a new way to better position yourself for a new opportunity.

Tactic: *Tell everyone you know*

Utilize your current design network to help make the transition. This is when the power of the network can really be seen. Designers are not just connected to other designers. You need to tell your network what you are looking for in order to start tapping into those deeper and less known connections.

Goal: Start a Business

Some people are born with the entrepreneurial gene; others develop the need to build something of their own years into their professional careers. During the 2008-2009 recession, the number of freelancers and consultants increased. Forced out of traditional employment, numerous interior designers resorted to offering their expertise as sole proprietors. Many did that just to get by; others found business ownership a comforting experience and continue on that path to this day.

Entrepreneurship can be a career choice. In fact, there are many interior designers who have packaged their services in new and unique ways and are successful business owners. Some formed unique collaborative companies. Others offer virtual design where they never actually meet the client or see the project site in person–all the work and communication happens online or over the phone. We know designers who focus their business on storytelling and branding. We have also seen designers find success in film and theater set production. No matter how you arrive at this entrepreneurial moment, there are many details to consider. Some people may need to meticulously plan and evaluate the pros and cons, while others just truly feel the entrepreneurial spirit and jump right in. As much as business ownership is a leap of faith and a commitment to a roller-coaster ride, there are certain aspects that require research and preparation.

1) Determining the Value Proposition

Tactic: *If you were to start a business, what would it be?*
Talk to other business owners and research similar businesses online. What kind of value are they promoting/offering to their clients? How will your business differ from theirs?

Tactic: *Try working for a business that resembles your business idea.*
It's less risky and costly to learn from someone else's successes and mistakes than your own. You may actually learn some things you did not consider before.

Tactic: *Write a business plan.*
Utilize trusted resources, such as U.S. Small Business Administration. The experience of writing a plan for your business can be intense, but it will address many areas you might have not been thinking about. For example: profit vs. loss, competition, delivery or distribution channels, and potential growth or growth limitations.

Tactic: *Clearly state your services.*
For website use or in printed collateral, comb through and condense lengthy blocks of content. No one has the time to read long paragraphs, so pick your words carefully. This will clearly communicate your business proposition and play a big role in the search engine optimization of your website and the various social media company channels. Remember that the general public may not know what an interior designer does, so help them understand.

Tactic: *Set up pricing.*
You may be hesitant about publishing your pricing structure but there are more benefits to it than not. It can serve as a filter for those who are interested in your service or product, but can't afford it. It will also help establish a transparent reputation for your brand.

2) Consider the Best Structure for Your Business

Tactic: *Get advice.*
Make an appointment with a local small business mentor or counselor through the U.S. Small Business Administration to learn the critical steps to start a business.

Tactic: *Protect your product, services and intellectual property.*
Make sure you are protecting your unique services and products through copyright, trademark or patent. Visit www.uspto.org for more information or get legal representation to guide you through the process. Hire a lawyer, if you are in a position to, to ensure the proper procedures are put into place.

Tactic: *Register the business.*
Select a business classification that best protects you and your employees (sole proprietorship, limited liability company, corporation, partnership, etc.)

Tactic: *Protect yourself.*
Research the type and the level of liability insurance you need to protect yourself and your customers, in case something goes terribly wrong. Contact your professional organization to see if it offers group insurance coverage. It's better to be safe than sorry.

Tactic: *Hire an accountant.*
Unless you have accounting experience, hire a certified accountant to help you manage the financial side of the business. Whether you are a sole proprietor or you have a team of people working for you, being able to hand off monthly billing and reporting will allow you to focus on the business and the clients (the reason you started the business in the first place). Remember when we discussed your

strengths and weaknesses in **Chapter 3 - The Brand of You**? Know what you're good at and what to pass on to others.

3) Develop Your Customer Base

Tactic: *Know who you are selling to.*
Create an ideal customer profile (demographic, socioeconomic status, location, niche market, what problem do they have that your product/service is solving?

Tactic: *Develop a marketing plan.*
Once you know who your ideal client is, select the best marketing platforms to reach that client. We shared numerous options in **Chapter 8 - Marketing**. Remember that networking and word of mouth are the most reliable, yet most time-consuming, marketing methods to develop.

Tactic: *Launch your website.*
Have a website made for your business. No excuses. Use a free template or a free service if you must. With time, you will be able to afford a custom Web page. Custom does not have to mean expensive. It simply means made to meet your needs.

Tactic: *Take full advantage of your website.*
Every page of your site should have a "call to action." Once potential clients land on that page, what do you want them to do next? One thing you don't want to happen is for them to bounce off your site or leave disengaged. After they read your content or watch a video, do you want them to share it, buy the product you are talking about or leave a comment? You should give them an easy way to do these things. Do you want them to sign up for a newsletter, free webinar

or download an e-book? Then you should give them an easy access to it. Do you want them to contact you with more questions? You should have your contact information available right there.

Constant Reinvention

The process of self-analysis, brand development and strategic career development is never finished. You will find yourself going through these steps again and again. And you have to be okay with it. Never think of a change as a failure. Change, solicited or unsolicited, is an opportunity–so adapt and move on. The world changes constantly; so do career paths and options. We must remain flexible to find continued success and happiness, as the days of holding a long-term position with one company from graduation to retirement are long gone. Maybe that's for the better. If we only have this one life, why not live it to the fullest? Why not experience many different work styles, employment opportunities and company cultures? Be ready for a lifetime of continued reinvention, improvement and growth.

Think About. . .

You can do this!

If you need a break, take one...but then get back to work on *The Brand of You*.

If you need a pep talk, contact one of us via LinkedIn - Subject: *The Brand of You Pep Talk*

Explore

On entrepreneurship or starting a business:
1. *The Girl's Guide to Starting Your Own Business: Candid Advice, Frank Talk, and True Stories for the Successful Entrepreneur* by Caitlin Friedman and Kimberly Yorio
2. *My So-Called Freelance Life: How to Survive and Thrive as a Creative Professional for Hire* by Michelle Goodman
3. *The 4-Hour Workweek: Escape 9-5, Live Anywhere and Join the New Rich* by Timothy Ferriss
4. *The Art of the Start 2.0. The Time-Tested, Battle-Hardened Guide for Anyone Starting Anything* by Guy Kawasaki
5. *Be Your Best Boss: Reinvent Yourself from Employee to Entrepreneur* by William R. Seagraves

On job search:
1. *Linchpin. Are You Indispensible?* by Seth Godin
2. *The Leap: Launching Your Full-Time Career in Our Part-Time Economy* by Robert Dickie

On reinvention:
1. *Leading Change* by John P. Kotter
2. *Switch: How to Change Things When Change Is Hard* by Chip Heath & Dan Heath
3. *Drive: The Surprising Truth About What Motivates Us* by Daniel H. Pink
4. *The Pathfinder: How to Choose or Change Your Career for a Lifetime of Satisfaction and Success* by Nicholas Lore

CHAPTER 10

All About You

I T TAKES TIME to build brand recognition, to create a lasting impression and develop a strong market presence. Think of it in years rather than weeks or days. Why not start building your brand now, today? If "now" means while you are still in school, do it. If "now" means upon graduation, do it. If "now" means two, five, 10 or 15 years into your career, do it. There is no better time than now. There is no room for excuses or procrastination in the career development process. No one will do it for you, and it will surely not handle itself. Why? Because this is all about you.

Your Commitment

A high level of commitment to yourself, to your job and to your career is key to your success. There is something to be said about a committed student. As we speak to students of interior design, we can determine very quickly who is and who is not "in it to win it." The standouts are inquisitive, energetic, yearn for more knowledge, turn assignments in on time and are ready for the next challenge. They always think if they had just a little more time their projects could be better. They find a way to balance their personal and professional responsibilities. They aren't the people falling asleep in class, always late or full of excuses.

"Don't be afraid to start at the bottom, even if it is not glamorous. You may not get put on the best or biggest project as a new designer, but every opportunity is a chance to learn—and that's how careers are built."

— Stacy Garcia
Founder/Chief Inspiration Office
Stacy Garcia Inc.—Nanuet, N.Y.

CAREER ADVICE FROM OUR CONTRIBUTORS

What is the best decision you made along the way to achieve your career success?

"To stretch myself. To take on responsibilities and push myself outside my comfort zone. I have done that throughout my career and continue to do it now."

— Bill Lyons, LEED AP, Assoc. AIA
Principal & Managing Director
Gensler-Minneapolis

———————◆———————

"Securing a really strong design foundation remains one of the strongest 'legs up' I feel I still possess versus many others in my field who came to the career by virtue of film school alone. However, I cannot distill a singular moment or specific decision to which I can attribute my success. I will say that listening to the voice that told me when everything wasn't right along the way was what allowed me to be successful. Recognizing what was wrong, analyzing and cataloging those lessons and then altering my path accordingly has been the singular THREAD that has brought me to the place where I can achieve success. Asking why things felt right or wrong, not stopping with things being just okay and not stopping until I had a course of action to make things right. I am in the right career for me, because I didn't stunt myself by trying to make 'me' right for all the wrong, but close to right, jobs. And in my design decisions, I have absolute confidence in the soundness of my designs, because of having to hone this process for so long just to GET to this career path— asking questions, justifying answers, analyzing and pushing through to make things right."

— Jessica Mahnke
Production Designer
Los Angeles

As a professional, your level of commitment is shown by your willingness to go that extra mile. Do you come in early or stay late when deadlines need to be met? Do you ask if anyone needs help when your work is done or before you head out the door for the night? Are you inspired by the world around you in way that work is always somehow on your mind?

"I would like to say there was one defining moment or thought, but that is not my history. Always a series of choices, chances, courage and sometimes setbacks, but moving forward."

— Ralph Ruder
Owner
Ralph Ruder Design–
Palm Springs, Calif.

◆

"To become involved in two key organizations, ASID and IFMA (International Facility Management Association). The network of people I connected with in both groups has been invaluable on a professional and personal level. My involvement exposed me to different types of professional careers for designers and a deeper understanding of the role of a facility manager within a company."

— Sandy Weber
Account Executive
MDC Wall–Milwaukee

◆

"To believe in myself and abilities—deciding NOT to listen to that negative inner voice when doubts crept in. I faced that choice often and had to decide each day that I was doing the right thing and had to keep moving forward, even if it was difficult."

— Michelle Goertz
Interior Designer
Dalton Steelman Arias &
Associates–Las Vegas

◆

"The best decision I made along the journey of my career was choosing to take a risk. The worst thing that could have happened is that it wouldn't work out. I am able to live with the risk of failure, but I would never be content with the idea of not trying. Of course, you should not dive into anything completely unprepared, so it is important to set yourself up for the best chance at success. Make a plan and set your goals. After that, all that is left to do is leap. Stretch outside the boundaries of your comfort zone. This is where growth will happen."

— Stacy Garcia
Founder/Chief Inspiration Office
Stacy Garcia Inc.–
Nanuet, N.Y.

We sometimes forget what true commitment means until the inevitable happens–you fail to follow up with a team member and you leave that person hanging, or worse yet, you miscommunicate with a client and under-deliver on his or her expectations. If you are not fully committed, feelings get hurt, tensions rise and bad memories are created. Those are hard to erase. When a perfect opportunity arises, you may not be the one to get the call. The calls will come to the professionals known for their dedication to the profession, their work ethic and their reliability.

Whether you graduated a month or 10 years ago, the level of commitment required to make it in this industry remains the same. How serious are you about succeeding? Are you willing to spend hours researching firms and designers you admire, products and projects that inspire, or reading materials that make you better at what you do? Are you as serious as spending a Sunday afternoon preparing for a project presentation instead of watching your favorite TV show (remember, that is what DVR is for)? No one else but you can set that bar.

Your Time

Between school, jobs, family and friends, hobbies and fun, who has the time and energy left for networking and building *The Brand of You*? We all have the same amount of time. Unfortunately, you can't buy more of it, nor can you save it for later. How you spend your time is entirely up to you. You choose whether to watch a reality show or research career opportunities. You decide if you are going to attend a networking event or go out dancing with friends. It is up to you whether to invest money in your education or to shop till you drop. Everyone says they are busy, but what does that really mean? We can easily fill a day, but are you filling your day with meaningful tasks and activities that support the success of *The Brand of You*?

Your Persistence

Are you a leader or a follower? When it comes to your life, you have to be the leader. Don't rely on or wait until your parents, teachers, coaches or friends tell you what to do next. While their thoughts and advice can be helpful, you have to make your own decisions. Why? You know, deep down, what's best for you. If it feels right to take a weekend off and fly across the country, do it. If you cringe at the thought of being chained to a cubicle and doing mundane tasks all day just to make ends meet, look for something else. If you think that volunteering at a local hospital will give you a better understanding of the healthcare industry, sign up today. Don't wait for someone to hand you your life plan. The longer you wait, the harder it will be to realize your dream. Don't fall into a trap of following someone else's plan. Make your own.

Focus on your voice within, listen to your intuition and go for it. Commit to your future, do your best, put in the time and the effort, and remain patient.

> *"There are days that you will doubt yourself, feel inadequate, get discouraged, and even cry. I've always thought the difference between those who give up and those who keep going just might be a good night's sleep. Have a good pity party; cry your eyes out if you must. Then put yourself to bed and rest. Recharge. A new day can bring new perspective. I always found the drive to pick myself up and dust myself off the next morning with a mind and spirit rested enough to attack the day's challenges."*

> — Michelle Goertz
> *Interior Designer*
> Dalton Steelman Arias & Associates–Las Vegas

Life has a funny way of working itself out. If you don't get that dream job immediately after graduation or even five or ten years later, don't give up. It may just be an unexpected turn on your road to success. If Thomas Edison had quit after his first rejection, we would never have experienced the convenience of a light bulb. His perseverance led him to succeed eventually. He famously said, *"I have not failed. I have just found 10,000 ways that won't work."* Every big success must experience its ups and downs. There will be bumps in the road, but if you are 100 percent committed, you will find another way.

Identifying your career goal and developing *The Brand of You* is hard work. You have to stick to it and consistently strive to reach your goal and build your brand one small step at a time (there is the level of commitment, again). Whatever it is, take our advice. You must persist to exist.

What You Want

Building a recognizable and reputable personal brand takes commitment, time and persistence. *Your* commitment. *Your* time. *Your* persistence. We hope this guide helps you achieve your goals, and we hope you succeed. But we can't do this for you. You are not alone on this journey, but this process is all about you and *The Brand of You*. Your career happiness will enrich your entire life, as well as the lives of others. So, what do you want? It is time for you to figure out who you are and what you want your life to be.

Good luck!

Think About. . .

Did you read this book from start to finish? If so, then what's next? Where are you in the brand building process? Return to the chapter that will help you get to the next level.

Did you take this book one chapter at a time? Are you reading this because you think you have reached the end...Think again! Even if you think you are happy in this career moment, anticipate what's next and think about – What if? What will your next move be? Prepare for it.

If you have a success story, please share it with us at myjourney@thebrandofyou.com

If you have a career challenge, please share it with us at myjourney@thebrandofyou.com

Explore

On drive and self-motivation:
1. *Drive* by Daniel Pink
2. *Crush It* by Gary Vaynerchuk
3. *Evil Plans: Having Fun on the Road to World Domination* by Hugh McLeod

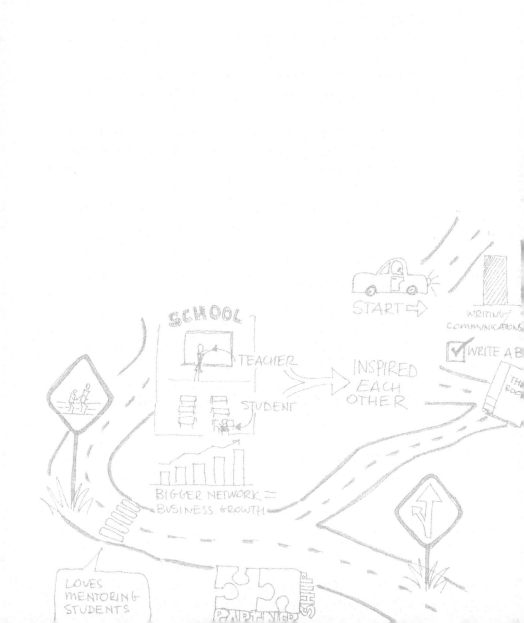

Notes

Chapter 2 The Fuel and The Factors

1 *2014-2015 Occupational Outlook Handbook*, United States Department of Labor, Bureau of Labor Statistics, January 8th, 2014 <http://www.bls.gov/ooh>

2 *Interior Design 2014 Outlook and State of The Industry*, American Society of Interior Designers, Page 12

3 *Interior Design 2014 Outlook and State of The Industry*, American Society of Interior Designers, Page 23

4 *2014-2015 Occupational Outlook Handbook*, United States Department of Labor, Bureau of Labor Statistics, January 8th, 2014 <http://www.bls.gov/ooh>

5 *Interior Design 2015/2016 Outlook and State of the Industry*, American Society of Interior Designers, Page 03

Chapter 3 The Brand of You

6 "The Brand Called You," Tom Peters, *Fast Company Magazine*, August 31st, 1997 <http://www.fastcompany.com/28905/brand-called-you>

7 *Now, Discover Your Strengths*, Marcus Buckingham and Donald O. Clifton, Chapter 2, Page 61

8 Ibid, Page 8

9   National Council for Interior Design Qualification website http://www.ncidqexam.org/about-ncidq/ hire-ncidq-certificate-holder/

Chapter 8 Marketing

10 LinkedIn Newsroom https://press.linkedin.com/about-linkedin

11 "Revolutionizing the world of recruiting" infographic by eBizMedia

12 Ibid.

13 LinkedIn Official Blog https://blog.linkedin.com

14 "The best and worst times to post on social networks" infographic by Social Caffeine

15 Pew Research Center http://www.pewinternet.org/2013/12/30/social-media-update-2013/

16 Facebook Newsroom http://newsroom.fb.com/company-info/

17 "The best and worst times to post on social networks" infographic by Social Caffeine

18 Pew Research Center http://www.pewinternet.org/2013/12/30/social-media-update-2013/

19 Twitter About https://about.twitter.com/company

20 "The best and worst times to post on social networks" infographic by Social Caffeine

21 Pew Research Center http://www.pewinternet. org/2013/12/30/social-media-update-2013/

22 Business Insider http://www.businessinsider.com/google-active-users-2015-1

23 Pew Research Center http://www.pewinternet. org/2013/12/30/social-media-update-2013/

24 YouTube Press Room https://www.youtube.com/yt/press/

25 YouTube – The 2nd largest search engine" infographic by Mushroom Networks http://www.mushroomnetworks.com/ infographics/youtube---the- 2nd-largest-search-engine-infographic

26 YouTube Official Blog http://youtube-global.blogspot. com/2013/05/yt-brandcast-2013.html

27 Pew Research Center http://www.pewinternet. org/2013/12/30/social-media-update-2013/

28 "The best and worst times to post on social networks" infographic by Social Caffeine

29 Instagram Press Room https://instagram.com/press/

30 Ibid.

ABOUT THE AUTHORS ➤

Aga Artka, ASID, NCIDQ, WRID

agaartka.com
linkedin.com/in/agaartka

Aga believes that every person and every business has a story to tell. Her own story is unlike most, as she immigrated to the US as a freshman in college in a search of an opportunity to do something great. Aga worked for small and large design companies and ended up starting an interior design practice of her own. As an interior designer, she utilizes her creativity to translate her clients' stories and brands into three-dimensional space.

Aga holds an Associate Degree in Interior Design from Milwaukee Area Technical College (MATC), NCIDQ Certification, LEED Professional Accreditation and is a Wisconsin Registered Interior Designer. She has been an independent interior design professional since 2009 and an active volunteer for the Wisconsin Chapter of American Society of Interior Designers (ASID). In 2008, she was recognized as Volunteer of the Year. She served as WI Chapter Professional Development Director from 2011-2013. Aga is the WI Chapter President for the 2015-2016 term.

Jenny Rebholz, Allied ASID

pushpointmarketing.com
linkedin.com/in/jennyrebholz

Jenny enjoys telling stories – stories about companies, projects, industry trends and people. As the Chief Connector and Creative Writer at PushPoint Marketing, she helps clients move beyond the pretty design pictures to identify the unique aspects of a project, share their industry expertise and differentiate themselves in the marketplace.

Jenny earned a Bachelor of Arts degree from the University of Wisconsin – Stevens Point with a double major in Interior Architecture and Communications. She worked for six years as an interior designer in both the Milwaukee and Phoenix markets before transitioning to the marketing side of the business. Jenny applies that hands-on knowledge as she works with clients to promote their companies.

From writing for industry publications such as design:retail and ASID's ICON and teaching in Milwaukee area interior design programs to volunteer work with the Wisconsin Chapter of ASID, Jenny has always found a way to support the future of the design profession.

CPSIA information can be obtained
at www.ICGtesting.com
Printed in the USA
LVOW04s0549050117

519792LV00006B/167/P